THE KOEHLER METHOD OF TRAINING TRACKING DOGS

Also by WILLIAM R. KOEHLER:

The Koehler Method of Dog Training
The Koehler Method of Guard Dog Training
The Koehler Method of Open Obedience for Ring, Home and Field (with Retrieving)
The Koehler Method of Utility Dog Training
The Wonderful World of Disney Animals

THE KOEHLER METHOD OF

TRAINING TRACKING DOGS

by

WILLIAM R. KOEHLER

Photography by
Sheldon W. Koehler

FIRST EDITION

New York

Macmillan General Reference
A Simon & Schuster Macmillan Company
1633 Broadway
New York, NY 10019-6785

Library of Congress Cataloging in Publication Data

Koehler, William R.
The Koehler method of training tracking dogs.

Bibliography: p. 144
1. Tracking dogs. 2. Dogs—Obedience trials—Tracking. 3. Dogs—Training. I. Title.
SF428.75.K64 1984 636.7′0886 84-10935
ISBN 0-87605-766-0

10 9

Printed in the United States of America

To the memory of
CARL SPITZ, Sr.,
a great dog trainer,
a true patriot and
a fine gentleman.

These dogs, trained in a class conducted by the author in 1957, earned their T's in the first test they entered. From left to right: Peggy Foster with Mike, U.D.T.; Carol Taylor with Topsy, U.D.T.; and Lucille Taylor with Hy-Ly, U.D.T. The judge is the late Carl Spitz. Lucille Taylor handled both the Bull Terrier and her Boxer to their "first test" successes in a single test, a record that still stands.
—Schley

Contents

About the Author

THE LIST is now complete. The Koehler training books (see Page 2), with their emphasis on sure, infallible performance in the face of any distraction, have been a giant influence in the continued advancement of American dog training. Now, with publication of this book, there is a Koehler guide for training your dog for every title in the American Kennel Club Obedience repertoire.

Great news, and most appropriate. Bill Koehler was, for many years, a very active and successful competitor with his own dogs at AKC Obedience trials, as well as helping others train their dogs. The Koehler training methods were shaped and honed out of this personal experience—a fact overshadowed in the glow of Bill's later fame as trainer of the Disney movie dogs.

Bill's background encompasses breeding, exhibiting, handling and training—with many breeds. Claire Bradshaw, of the superintending family, writes of the important part that a white Bull Terrier, bred and trained by Bill Koehler, played in her children's growing up.

In the later 1940s, after service as a war dog trainer, Bill became the Obedience spark for many southern California clubs. He conducted training classes and was Obedience Trial Chairman for the Orange Empire Dog Club, the largest open membership dog club in the United States. He led Obedience classes at the Boxer Club of Southern California, and at the Doberman Pinscher Club of Southern California, and was instructor for the Field Dog classes at the Irish Setter Club of Southern California, which were open to all pointing breeds.

Since 1947, over 21,000 dogs have gone through Obedience training in classes under his supervision. The number of Obedience and Tracking titles and the dazzling percentage of Highest in Trial awards won by these dogs is its own testimony to the effectiveness of his training methods.

Many other honors speak for his authority. Three movie dogs he trained won the annual Patsy award of the American Humane Association.

He organized the first comprehensive temperament testing program in California in 1957, won many academic citations as head of the Foundation for the Applied Study of Animal Behavior, and has been saluted by veterinary and humane organizations for his work in saving problem dogs from destruction. He owns commendations from the Division of Veterinary Medicine of the U.S. Army and from the Canadian Police Canine Association. He has been sought as a consultant by District Attorneys and by the Department of Justice, and holds status as an expert witness in California, Wisconsin and Hawaii.

Bill Koehler's keen knowledge of dog motivation, together with his genius for training, find ideal blend in THE KOEHLER METHOD OF TRAINING TRACKING DOGS. If your aim is to train your dog for a T.D. or T.D.X. title, or to track lost people or do police work, this is the book for you.

ACKNOWLEDGMENTS

IT WOULD BE impractical to list the names of all of you who supplied feedback and other favors needed for this book, but I trust that all of you will see your contributions reflected in its pages and sense my deep appreciation for your kindness.

— Bill Koehler

1

A Realistic Foundation

WHETHER you are first considering the subject of tracking or have trained and handled a dog to a T.D. (Tracking Dog) or T.D.X. (Tracking Dog Excellent) title, this book will offer some new opportunities for your satisfaction and pleasure.

If your aim is for a dog that will provide the casual fun of tracking and, more importantly, regard the presence of animals and other distractions as reasons why he should concentrate more intently on the track of a lost child, this book will point the way.

If you have believed that training your dog to track was limited to only awakening and encouraging your dog's natural abilities, and you've watched him bomb in a half dozen trials because he needed something more than "natural desires," this book can show you a realistic approach to the problem.

Because it covers areas relating to tracking-dogs that other works have omitted, the book will be of value both to readers who will use it as a manual and to all those who wish to increase their knowledge of dogs at work.

The author suggests that you read the book from beginning to end before you use it as a manual. You will then follow it with the utmost confidence because you will know that each step reasonably prepares the way for the next. Follow the instructions carefully. Don't mix the book's philosophy. Hybridizing produces good seed corn, but lousy dog training methods.

These dogs will be worked on a leash and line until they are totally free of contention around distractions.

For many years all of the hundreds of dogs that have participated in the Open Classes sponsored by The Orange Empire Dog Club have been required to retrieve dumbbells, placed close to unusual distractions, as part of their realistic training. This is to prepare them for the certainty that they will encounter temptations while working in the obedience ring or on a track.

Those of you who used *The Koehler Method of Open Dog Training* as a text for training your dog to retrieve are aware of the carefully scheduled increments it describes to instill such reliability before the course of twelve weeks is completed. Uninformed trainers have sometimes criticized the above book's progressions for "taking too long"; but to see even the most shy and reluctant dogs retrieve reliably and happily by the end of the course has convinced the thousands who have closely followed the book that the method is infallible.

The pictures on this and the facing page illustrate simple tests that can tell you whether you and your dog are prepared to get the maximum benefit from the book you hold, which emphasizes the use of positive retrieving as the best motivation.

The value of the blind-retrieve to some of the exercises in Utility Work has been demonstrated to many thousands of people in clinics

The more confusion the better during the on-leash level of training.

By the end of an Open Course all of the dogs should retrieve reliably around informal situations and distractions.

I have conducted in most areas of the United States, Canada and other countries. They have seen how easy it is to cause positively motivated dogs to responsibly seek and retrieve objects that were hidden from sight. These dogs were strangers to me, and the only condition imposed was that before the demonstrations they retrieve in proximity to the distractions that are used at all my clinics and seminars, so all present would know they were positive retrievers.

If these thousands of people had any questions as to whether positively motivated dogs worked more reliably than dogs that were trained "inducibly" or were no more than "natural retrievers" that question was soon answered. How?

Because the handlers of the inducibly trained and "natural retrievers" were always offered equal opportunity to work their dogs and, with one or two exceptions refused, it must be concluded that their convictions had withered in the heat of reality.

This tracking-book is not intended as an aid to training a dog to retrieve, but it should mention that there are various ways to train and motivate a dog to retrieve under challenging conditions.

But there is only one way of testing the merit of any method, and that is to see how dogs it trains respond under new and distracting conditions. If they fail to respond to one command, the speed and attitude of proper response to correction will reveal whether they were realistically trained.

You will soon see how this test can relate to a dog's reliability on a track.

Many dedicated individuals have studied everything they can relate to the dog's unique scenting powers and have recorded many observations. They have used written instructions and elaborate diagrams to help in an effort to arouse and develop the tracking ability in dogs. The purveyors of this material seem to agree in chorus that, "We humans cannot track by scent and know little of scent's mysteries, so obviously there is no positive way we can make a dog use his ability to track."

"This being true," the refrain continues, "there is no way to correct a dog if he goldbricks, is distracted, or for other reasons fails to track naturally—one must use only patient repetition, encouragement, or tidbits until the pump is primed and sufficient desire is aroused to keep him motivated in the face of distractions and difficulties he might encounter on the track." Often a believer has used varied techniques in this "pump priming" to arouse the "latent desire," and then depended solely on that desire to motivate a dog as he sought to sharpen his ability on complex tracks. Tidbits used in various ways have been combined with games of "hide-and-seek" and other gimmicks in order to hype the dog into expressing his natural ability and bring about some degree of success. Pleasure for both handler and dog has been derived from such healthy outdoor recreation, and from participating in tracking trials. "After all," some of the enthusiasts echo, "the dog is only doing what comes naturally. It has to be fun—you can't make him do it. To correct him for mistakes would make him quit, maybe for good."

But often there comes a day when one of those dogs is asked to track a lost person, and is doing his thing "naturally," when the track crosses an area where wild animals have played about. This is true when a dog, motivated only by his free choice of things to do, and who might even have the credential of a "T", is called upon to trail a lost child whose track originated in a food-sprinkled picnic area,

When a track originates in a food-sprinkled picnic area and leads into a game-scented primitive area, you'll be glad your dog is motivated by more than food and "doing what comes naturally."

and leads into an animal-scented primitive area. Now any tidbit on the trail becomes a "natural" fueling stop. He finishes his snack and if he does pick up the track that leads into the brush, he "naturally" wants to investigate the hot scents of rabbits that have played their bunny games over all the paths the child could have followed. His handler, though naive in the matter of motivation, knows that the small, round droppings in which the dog has a "natural" interest were not deposited by a child, at least not a "natural" child. The handler stands prayerfully in that natural setting as the breeze blows through the brush with the haunting refrain: "There is no way to correct for failures. Don't correct—he'll quit."

Occasionally a handler, frustrated by such a moment of truth, will react strongly. Believing that what his dog has been doing for fun he should do as a duty, he will resort to switching or other means to instill the sense of responsibility that should have been instilled with a logical progression of steps. There are some rare dogs that will respond to such a demand for an instant metamorphosis, changing from a creature who does his thing naturally to a serious worker who is motivated by responsibility. But at best such attempts to instill instant responsibility depend more on luck than understanding and are a poor substitute for a logical approach.

There is no outside area where a dog can track without encountering distractions. Some handlers hope that luck will rule out the specific things that would tempt their dogs. They are the handlers who have never met the problems by instilling a positive motivation. There are others who want a practical tracker and must motivate their dogs in a way that will cause them to regard all the distractions on a trail as reasons to concentrate on the responsibility to track.

The motivation we will use will make the dog responsible for following a track in order to find and retrieve objects that bear a tracklayer's scent. DO NOT CONFUSE THIS WITH THE FREE-CHOICE "NATURAL RETRIEVING" WHERE THE DOG PERFORMS AS LONG AS THERE IS NOTHING ELSE HE WOULD "NATURALLY" DO AT THE MOMENT. The difference is great. It is the difference between the young dog who "naturally" runs out to get a bird he has seen fall, and the positively motivated dog who might have to go by the bird he sees and take the handler's direction to a bird he does not see.

Review the pictures on Pages 14 and 15 of dogs being trained in this positive retrieving. Such training is done in a kind and confidence-building way, with corrections justified by a dog's complete understanding at each level. Such an effective and humane program is in contrast to the unintentional cruelty of a handler who believed that his dog would do it all naturally, with no force applied, and then, when his dog fails to perform, believes that what the dog has done "naturally" is a foundation upon which he can justify a correction.

The pictures mentioned will describe a good test of readiness for you and your dog. When your dog will retrieve reliably under the conditions shown, you should be able to train him to follow tracks that would confuse or frustrate a "fun and games dog."

After your dog has a good foundation, give him practice in finding and retrieving objects on a track, such as those in the picture. Articles of many different kinds are sometimes dropped on a track by a lost person or a fugitive.

This is one kind of tracking-harness. The harness should be comfortable, but it is not necessary to hunt extensively for a certain style. For many years sled dogs, guide dogs and horses have pulled in harnesses that put pressure high on their chests without causing difficulty, so don't feel that any special harness will be a motivating factor.

EQUIPMENT

HARNESS: Obviously a good harness is much more suitable for tracking than even a wide collar would be. To resolve any questions as to the best type of harness, one could hardly do better than refer to the experience of persons who drive draft animals. They generally agree that the most efficient harness is the one that best distributes the pull across the animal's chest without restricting movement or constricting tightly on the rib cage. Whether you buy a harness or have a leather worker make one to your design, remember that soon your dog will be pulling on a line. Think of his comfort and endurance.

LINE: A line 40 feet long will serve for starting your dog in tracking. Also, it will meet regulations if you decide to get a tracking title on your dog. Later when we get into some phases of practical tracking you might want to make some changes to meet the demands of the area in which your dog will have to work. There are many light lines with ample strength to meet the pull of a dog in harness; and there is some advantage in a line of small width because there will be a minimal effect from strong winds and the drag of grass and brush. Some of the small diameter nylon lines are good, but there is a flat nylon line about three-eighths of an inch in width that feels better. And how important is the feel? It is important to any exercise of skill. That's why anthropologists are consulted on the design of controls in vehicles.

WIND FLAGS: You will need some stakes for your wind flags, and the best stakes are pieces of light concrete reinforcing rod or other metal rod. Such material is available at all building material dealers and some hardwares. They'll probably cut it for you into suitable lengths of from two to four feet, depending on the terrain and cover in which you will train. Such steel stakes are easily pushed into the ground and won't splinter on a rock. A bit of bright ribbon tied to the top of the stakes will help you mark a track and indicate the direction of any air movement.

Socks of all sizes and colors are easy to obtain. They are convenient for the tracklayer to carry, and he can use them to mark turns by tying a knot or using a significant color.

ARTICLES: For early training a dozen discarded socks that have been laundered since worn will serve as articles that can be dropped by the tracklayer.

DISTRACTIONS: In preparation for the time when you will place distractions on the track, you might make a list of some small animals that can be caged, and tempting scents that will be available to you.

2

Basic Patterns

LEVEL 1

Objective: Scent Association

One of your convenient small areas will do nicely for the start. However, it must have enough ground-cover to conceal small objects from your dog's view until he's within a few feet of them, yet permit you to see them at a greater distance from your higher viewpoint.

Equip your dog with his leash and training collar, and carry the tracking harness to a point where you and your helper will start work. You can make the introduction to his new responsibility easy if you use a simple preliminary before your dog is started on a track. Have your tracklayer take one of the socks from the sack and place it inside his shirt and leave it for a few minutes so that it will become thoroughly saturated with his scent. Now take the sock from him and place it in your dog's mouth as you start to teach him that all objects which bear a tracklayer's scent are things he must find and retrieve. Praise him lavishly for accepting it.

Don't worry about a bit of your own scent getting on the sock. As training progresses and your dog is retrieving all manner of objects that a tracklayer has dropped, these things will always bear his scent in combination with a variety of other scents. These would include the distinctive odors of clothing, soap and personal items together with the odors of soil and ground cover where an object is dropped. *But always in all these combinations there will be the*

Have your tracklayer place one of the socks inside his shirt for a few minutes to pick up his scent.

Place the sock in your dog's mouth as you start to teach him that all objects that bear a tracklayer's scent are things he must find and retrieve.

Be fair. Have him make a few short reaches for the scented sock.

—add a few longer reaches.

—and then have him make some blind retrieves from the concealment of grass.

tracklayer's personal scent, so there is no reason to worry that he'll be confused when your own scent is no longer on the objects. This truth holds even if your dog was previously trained in scent discrimination.

Repeat the introduction several times so that you'll be sure he's relating your command to the correct object. It is at this point that the introduction ceases and the dog is assigned a responsibility that will become his motivation to track to the best of his ability under all conditions. Now that he knows what you want him to fetch, have him make three or four arm-length reaches for the sock. Praise him lavishly. Next, face the dog into any air movement and put him on a down-stay. Place the sock in the grass about six feet in front of him. Wait a minute, then send him.

Don't let the fact that he's being sent from the down position, nor the short wait, cause you to excuse him if he fails to respond to your first command. Do not repeat the command, nor coax. Correct him just as you would for any failure to retrieve. Remember, you will gain by meeting any challenge the dog will offer early in his training, while he is close enough for effective corrections if any are needed. Repeat the pattern a few times, or until the dog is performing smoothly. It makes no difference that he now knows the location of the sock: whether or not he needs to seek for the sock, his awareness of the scent combination will be increased.

Now we'll call on your helper. Have him stand facing you on the spot where you've been placing the sock. Put your dog on the down-stay. Step out and drop the sock at the helper's feet. Return to the dog and send him. It is vital that you do not excuse the dog if he seems momentarily confused by the sight and scent of your helper. The sock is there! Correct just as you would for any failure to retrieve because of distractions. Five such retrieves, rewarded by sincere praise, should prepare your dog for the next small step.

Your helper should now take another sock from the sack and "scent it up" as he did first, which will positively identify it for your dog as an object he must retrieve. The positions of your dog and helper should be the same as they were for the last series of retrieves. The helper should drop the sock at his feet and stand quietly. He should not flourish the sock, chortle, or in other ways try to "show the dog." This is not "make-a-game" retrieving. You're assigning a responsibility that will motivate your dog to do an important job;

Have your tracklayer stand on the spot where you've been placing the sock. Place the sock at his feet and send the dog as explained in the text.

one which will give him a much deeper satisfaction than he could get from play.

Give your fetch-command. The fact that your dog might not have noticed your helper drop the sock is no reason for a second command or cue to retrieve. He must go in the direction he's sent whether or not he sees the object of the retrieve.

Instill full responsibility when the distances are short, so your dog will be past contention and enjoying his work when the distances are greater and handling more difficult. Correct him all the way to the sock if he doesn't respond. As is true in any situation that involves positive retrieving, don't be outmaneuvered by a dog that waits until the correction is about to start, then scuttles out to retrieve. Don't try to motivate him with threat. Motivate him with inevitability. If he waits, help him wait. Hold him back as you apply the justified correction until he is working hard to take you to the sock. It's rare that a positive retriever would hesitate in such a simple task, but you must be prepared to react in a positive manner.

Most likely your dog will respond favorably to your first command and give you the chance to heap the praise on him.

Repeat the pattern a half dozen times. Praise enthusiastically, even though the exercise seems below the ability of your positive retriever. You'll know you have been fair and have prepared him to work a short track.

Your dog's first track will be another step toward his full realization that he must use his nose in order to find and pick up any object that bears the tracklayer's scent.

When you've selected an area, set the starting flag yourself so it won't bear the tracklayer's scent. Stay back with your dog 50 feet or so, while your tracklayer scuffs a starting mark a couple of feet to the side of the flag.

The tracklayer should now walk with short steps directly into the wind for a distance of 30 feet, then turn around to face the starting point, and drop the sock at his feet.

Heel your dog to within a leash length of the starting point. Put the harness on him. During the early levels of his experience, the harness will serve only as one more part of a pattern that will tell him it's time to concentrate on tracking. Until instructed differently, work him with your leash and training collar even though he's

The tracklayer should scuff a starting mark near the flag you've set.

The tracklayer should walk about thirty feet, turn to face the flag, and drop the sock at his feet.

wearing the harness. Now move up to the point where the track starts and place him on the down-stay in line with the track, so that his nose is near the center of the scuff marks. Keep him on a down-stay for at least two minutes.

WHY THAT LONG? WATCH HIM, AND YOU'LL SEE. We don't know everything about the faculty of memory, but we're sure of one thing. Repetition does have some value. When a dog is on a down-stay, he'll check and recheck all of the smells that are available to his restricted area because there's little else to do. His nose is centered in the tracklayer's ground scent, and he'll double check it repeatedly, which means he'll recognize and memorize it more certainly. He'll soon learn that it's one of the combination of scents that can lead him to the objects the tracklayer has dropped and which he must seek. *Don't worry if his nose doesn't go clear to the ground—he'll still catch the scent.*

Follow the "memorizing time" with your usual command to retrieve. Later you can switch to a command relating better to tracking, but there's no hurry. Even when he's using a track to guide him to objects, a command to "Fetch" or "Take It" is still meaningful to him.

Chances are good that he'll go from the down-stay straight to the feet of the tracklayer to get the sock. Move up smoothly and quickly to where he picks up the sock, take it from him; and be quick to praise. Obviously any failure to complete such a simple task would merit correction.

Hold it, please! Don't tell me that he used the familiar form of the tracklayer as a cue to where the sock would be. I'm aware of that. Possibly you are not aware of some other things that occurred when he went to the sock. More of that same ground scent he had "memorized" radiated from the path the man had walked. It was combined with the man's body scent as he moved forward into the wind. Yes, he saw the man, but he didn't shut his nose off as he moved along. He was conscious of that beam of odors that was on the path to the sock. That association, repeated often enough, will convince him that track-scent can lead him to objects that the tracklayer has dropped. Your job is to supply the "often enough." Run him over a similar track a few times. Follow the complete pattern from the laying of the track to the praise for success.

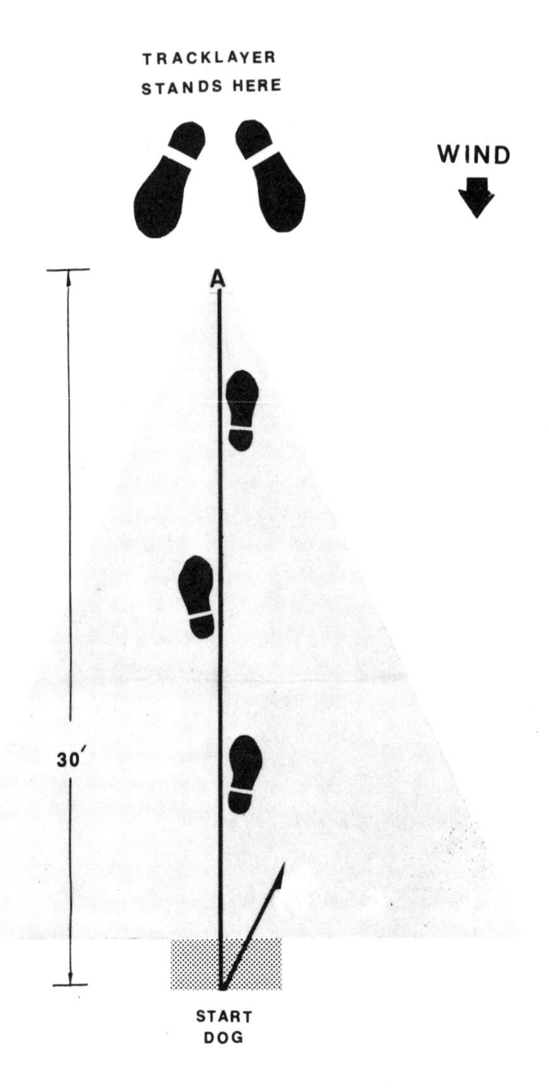

This drawing shows how the wind moves the spreading scent-cone towards your dog, funneling him into the combination of scents that relate to the track.

Senseless as it seems, this easy task will strengthen the association. Then remove his harness and take him from the area.

While you take a break, let's think about placing flags.

Anyone aware of the strong sense of responsibility a positively motivated retriever possesses will immediately understand why someone other than the tracklayer should place all flags used to mark the start or the course of a track. A realistically trained retriever, charged with the responsibility of identifying and retrieving and picking up any object that bears a tracklayer's scent, will feel he should pull a flag that carries the tracklayer's scent from the ground. To compound the error of a tracklayer placing flags is the fact that such scent would be higher off the ground, and could be airborne to the dog more strongly than the scent of articles on the ground. Forget about any idea of a rubber glove keeping the tracklayer's scent from a stake that he carries and sets. Contact or proximity could allow his body scent to permeate the stake or flag.

The placing of flags by another will pose no problem. He can easily place the flag to indicate where the tracklayer should start a

A responsible retriever will feel that he should retrieve any object on a track that bears a tracklayer's scent. Don't have the tracklayer set any flags.

A tracklayer can drop a sock, knotted a certain way or of a certain color, to mark a turn. Such "evidence" will be easy for your dog to retrieve and you to carry.

track. If any other flags are needed, he can walk in on a right angle to the course, or you can set the flags yourself well ahead of track-laying time. Now please—no tears of worry that someone else's scent might drift over where the track will be laid. Your dog will not be asked to follow the flag setter's track, and if he tried to, would be subject to correction. So no "oooh, oooh, ooohs."

In situations where it is more practical for your tracklayer to mark a change of course, or another feature, have him use a distinctive colored sock or other object that means "turn," or gives other information. If you're working in a brushy area, he can hang the marker on a bush. Not only will it be reasonable for the dog to retrieve such "evidence," it will be easier for you to carry than flags that would be retrieved because they bear the tracklayer's scent.

After a couple of hours of break time, bring your dog back to the area. Have your helper lay a new 10-yard track, proceeding just as he did when he set up the first track. Once again, bring your dog close to the starting point and put the harness on him. Move up, and down him with his nose over the scuff marks at the start of the track.

The nature and density of the scent combination can vary with the ground cover, humidity and temperature. The second track, even though close to the first one, could show your dog that changes can quickly occur. Concentrate on the purpose of the exercise, and handle consistently, as you give your dog a half-dozen experiences on similar 30-foot tracks. Call it a day when you've praised him for his last ridiculously easy performance. Do not "turn him loose for a run" in the tracking environment. Remove the harness and take him from the field for a bit of quiet time before he goes back to his everyday affairs. "Let him soak," as a horse trainer would say.

Second Day:

Work your dog on six more 30-foot tracks, proceeding exactly as you were instructed to do on the first day. The almost mechanical way in which he responds to the pattern will show you he's ready for the next level.

LEVEL 2. First Day.

Objective: To follow a track 30 feet long and pick up two objects, without presence of tracklayer. Track should be about a half-hour old.

Start the day with a bit of review. Have your tracklayer lay a track that's similar in all details to those used in the previous session, including the presence of the tracklayer. Your dog will probably move along more swiftly than before, so be sure to follow fast enough to keep unreasonable tension off the training collar. Although you put the harness on your dog, do not hook your leash to it. Don't even fasten the snap to the collar's "dead ring." Just move along fast enough to take the sock from him when he picks it up. As always, praise him for his success.

It is now time to make two significant changes. Put your dog back in the car or otherwise confine him so that he cannot see the tracking area. Have the tracklayer take two socks from your bag and scent them. He will then lay another 30-foot track, but this time drop one sock at the halfway point and the other at the end of the track. He should now take a giant step at a right angle from the track, so that the scent of the sock will be closer and stronger than the ground-scent that leads away from it. More long steps should take him cross wind until he's 50 feet from where he dropped the second sock; then

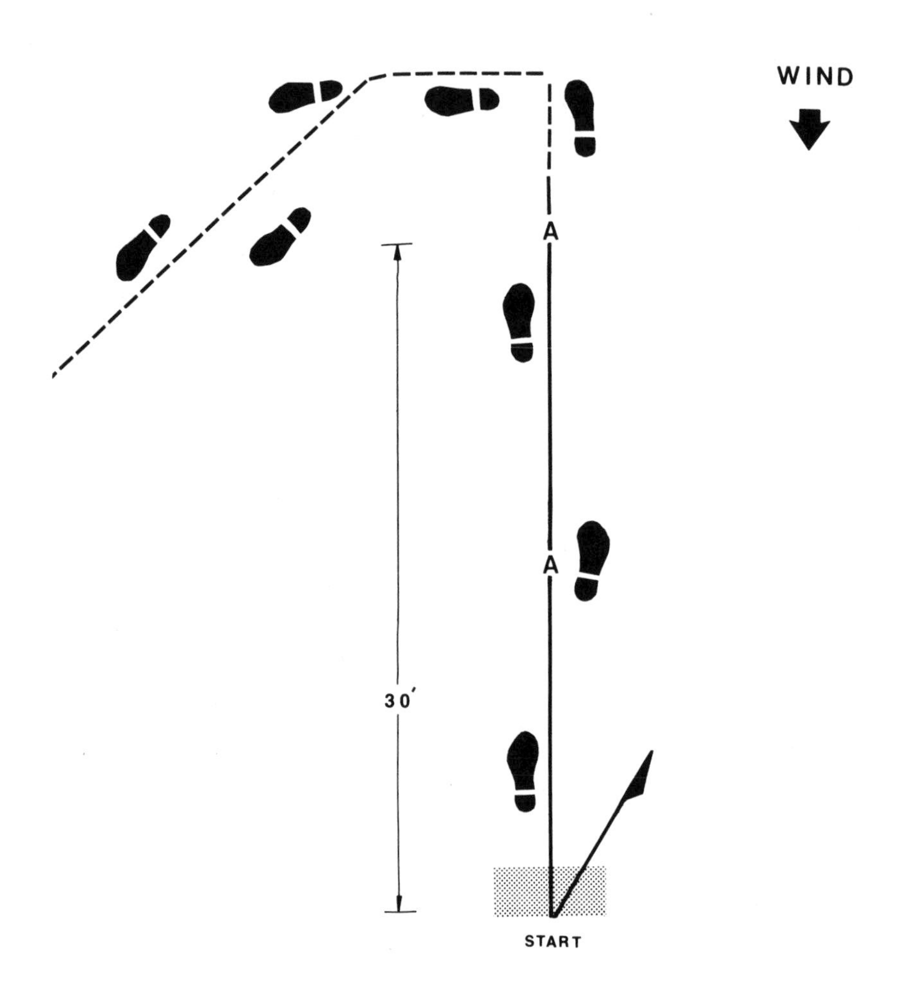

The solid line shows how the tracklayer lays a thirty foot track into the wind, spacing two socks as he goes. The broken line shows how he leaves the track, so his departure scent will not be blown to the dog.

he can double back to watch the proceedings from a place where his familiar form will not be visible to the dog.

Give the man's body scent a half-hour to blow off of the track before you bring the dog to the starting place. As usual, put the harness on the dog and place him on a down-stay with his nose over the scuff marks. Wait two minutes then give him the command to retrieve, and be ready to move quickly. There's a very small possibility that, since there is no visible tracklayer nor strong scent, the dog might hesitate. In such a case, do not give a second command or cue, even though he might appear confused. Correct him all the way to the first sock, and don't stop until he picks it up. You'll make a bad mistake if you let him feel it's safe to wait for a second command before he starts his effort. Whether or not he went without a correction, praise him when he lifts the sock, take it from him, and *quickly conceal it in your pocket* so he won't grab for it when he's commanded to follow his nose to the second sock.

Immediately face him in the direction the track goes and indicate the ground just past the point where he picked up the first sock. He'll already have the scent memorized and should move out promptly on your command. Obviously, if he seems to feel his job was done when he trailed to the one sock, and doesn't move out, you'll correct him all the way to the second sock. He probably moved right out without any need for correction, but in either case, give him lots of praise when he lifts the sock. Now, leave the end of the track at a right angle opposite the direction in which the tracklayer left.

Yes, I know that the tracklayer left ground scent when he jumped away from the upwind track he had laid, but there was nothing abortive about ending the tracking problem when the dog had the success and satisfaction of finding the second sock. Later, in practical tracking, there could be times when a track could end abruptly when the person tracked gets into a car. *The fact that your dog's motivation is the responsibility to retrieve makes him feel rewarded when he earns praise by finding the article.*

Take your dog from view of the area while your helper lays a fresh track, proceeding in all details as he did for the previous one. Give your helper's body scent time to dissipate, then start your dog. The requirements for your handling and the dog's performance will be the same as on the previous track.

You will notice when you start him that his attention goes to the ground scent without the high-headed scouting he did when the body scent was strong and the man in sight. You can bet he won't overshoot the first sock, and that when you've praised him, he'll move out again on one command to find the sock at the track's end.

Finish the day with four new tracks which should be duplicates of the one your dog worked. Your dog's performance should convince you that his work meets the objective given for this level of training.

Second Through Fourth Day

Before you begin the next day of training, I'm going to ask you to concentrate while I explain something that's very important but could appear trivial unless you understand it fully. I'm going to ask you to work your dog on a half dozen of those simple 30-foot tracks each day for the next three days. Stay with this familiar length and the pattern of socks, but use a new track each time. You might protest that the dog handles the tracks so mechanically that he seems almost in a groove. Right. We want that groove in which he's earned so much praise to be there for orientation during the next level of training, when you will supply the first of many experiences that will cause him to regard all distractions as reasons to turn his mind back to his work. So be sure to give him the suggested number of 30-foot tracks before you attempt the next level of training.

LEVEL 3

Objective: To increase the dog's concentration through the use of distractions.

The effective use of distractions is an essential part of any reasonable training course, so it is probable you've given your dog previous experience in rejecting temptations during his early obedience training, and the principle of using distractions to make a dog concentrate more intensely on his job will not be new to you. You will gain by applying the same principle directly in the tracking situation.

Realistically, the distractions your dog will encounter on tracks will be the scents of animals and food. Even on the edge of a city, almost every field will be traversed by small wild animals, and any

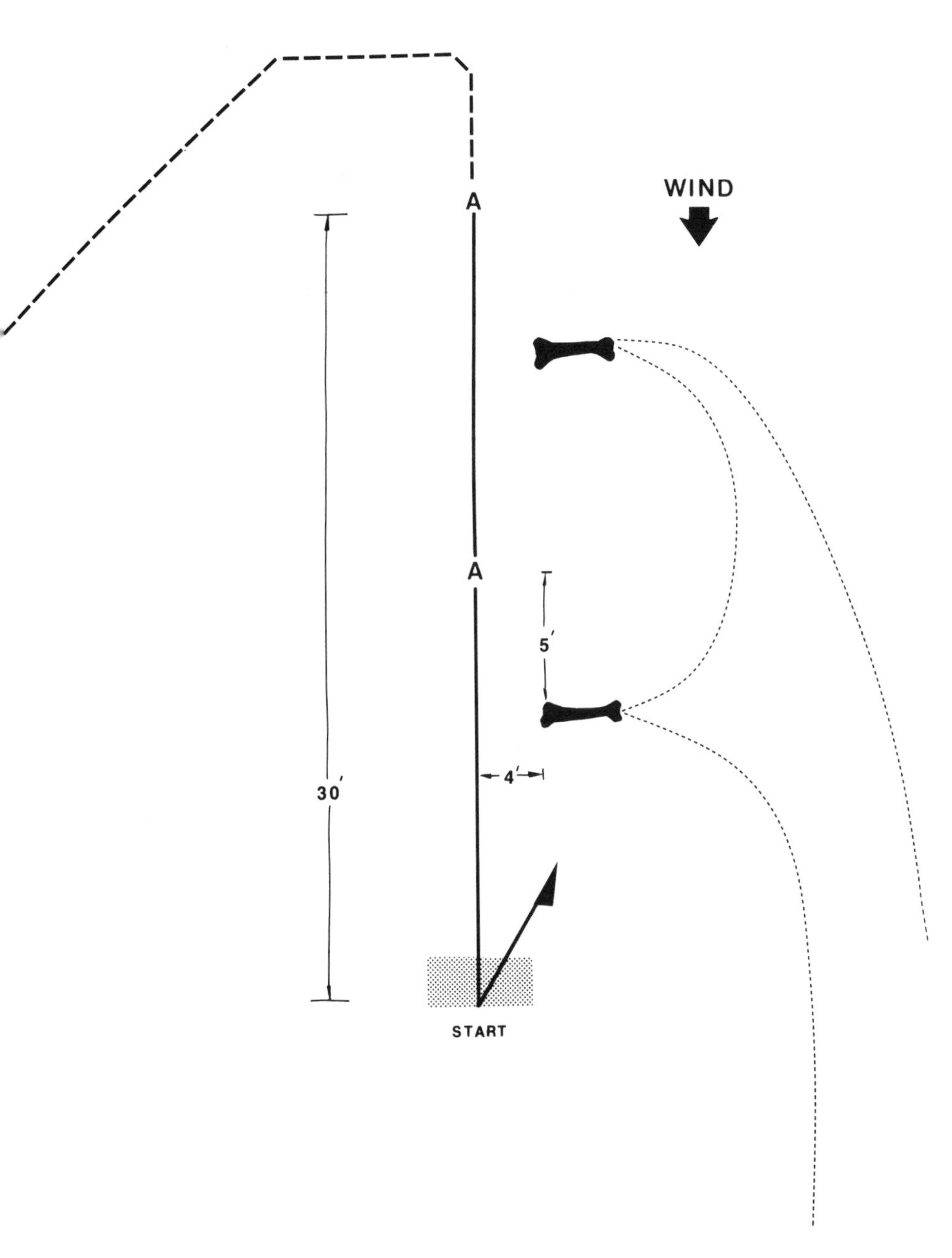

The light line shows how someone other than the tracklayer moves in to place the distractions in relation to the track and articles. The "bones" symbolize the distractions described in the text.

track that leads from a park or camp area is apt to have scraps of food. You must proof your practical tracker against such common items.

Distractions will occur naturally at varying distances and in unpredictable places on most tracks, but for our purpose it is advisable to stage the temptations so you can anticipate and observe your dog's reactions and make productive corrections if you should need to, and to praise the dog when he holds to his responsibility to track on by them. For convenience and to establish a pattern for the dog to start a track responsibly and carefully, stage your distractions on a 30-foot track.

You can protect and control animal distractions with a small cage. Enclose food temptations in cheesecloth or a cotton sack so you can make a correction if your dog decides it's safe to try and eat what he finds on a track instead of rejecting it as a practical tracker should. The tracklayer must not touch the distractions as they would then bear his scent, which would be unfair to the dog. It will make no difference if you should touch them, even if your dog is trained in scent discrimination. Your scent is not the one your dog will be asked to follow. But if you should place them, stay off the track, and move in from the side to set them.

Have the tracklayer lay another one of those simple 30-foot tracks with a sock at the halfway point and another at the end. When he's finished and retired to a place downwind of the starting point, place the distractions. Approach the track from the side and set one of the objects about 4 feet off the track and about 5 feet before your dog will reach the first sock. Now step away from the track and move up to a point 5 feet before the second sock and place the second distraction 4 feet off the track as was described for the first setup. The drawing on Page 39 will show you the relationship of distractions and socks.

Allow a half hour for body scents to clear the tracks before you start your dog. Be ready to do some fast and flawless handling as your dog approaches the first distraction. Even if the track is going directly into the wind, the spectrum of scent from the distractions should be wide enough to reach the dog before he detects the sock. It will be natural for your dog to alert on the tempting scent and take a moment to check its source.

If he then goes on by and finds the sock, heap loads of praise on him. But if his pause is extended to a longer time and he shows his attention has been diverted from his responsibility to track, act fast. Snatch him away from the distraction and correct him all the way to the sock. Praise him for the pickup. Give him the command to resume work.

Handle the second distraction exactly as you did on the first. Praise when he rejects the temptations: correct if he goofs. Work three more tracks similar to the first. If your dog was made to perform around strong distractions when you were training him to retrieve, you will soon see him adapt a "get-thee-behind-me" attitude, and concentrate more intensely on his job when he encounters temptations on a track. Even though he speedily reaches that favorable attitude, continue to work on similar distraction-setups on each of four consecutive days so that the very familiarity reminds him to concentrate on his job.

The recommended four days of work will give you concentrated practice in observing your dog's reactions when he detects and rejects a distraction or when he shows he is preoccupied with it. And your dog will become very conscious that you can read him like a book.

This practice will help to prepare the two of you for tracks where your dog will face chance distractions that you won't be able to see.

If you have one of those rare dogs that doesn't want to start down "the tunnel of truth" where he experienced some discomfort, the problem is easily solved. Correct him swiftly past the distraction and on to the first sock. Keep emotion out of the correction but put a lot of it into the praise you'll give him for picking up the sock. Chances are he'll start fast on your command to hit the trail for the second sock. By now your dog has earned heaps of praise for tracking past distractions and picking up articles the tracklayer has dropped. Now you and your dog are ready for the challenge and satisfaction of the next level.

LEVEL 4

Objective: Reliability on a 50-foot track into the wind.

First Day:

You or another person than the tracklayer should stake the start and finish of a track about 10 feet longer than the previous tracks you've used. It's easy to place the first flag, but care must be used in placing the second so no one but the tracklayer walks on the track course at this level of training. As before, the tracklayer should drop one sock at the halfway point and another at the finish where he will leave at the usual crosswind angle. At the time of this change do not stage deliberate distractions, but, should a chance temptation divert your dog's attention, be prepared to correct him to a sock. Let the track age half an hour or so before you bring your dog to the scuff marks and start him.

The slight increase in track length will allow more time for wind shifts; and it's important for you to watch the wind direction so you'll understand if your dog slows down momentarily to work things out.

The third track of the day should be 50 feet in length.

Second Day:

Work three of the 50-foot tracks into the wind.

SUMMARY

You have been working your dog on tracking for at least twelve days. You have developed a motivation in your dog to follow a track 50 feet long that will lead him into the wind to find objects that were dropped by the tracklayer. It's now time for you to do a bit of summarizing, and for me to answer some questions you might have before we go on to longer and more complex tracks.

By now, your dog takes the unvarying pattern of being brought to the trackhead on leash, and there being equipped with a harness that so far is only a symbol, then being placed on a down for two minutes on the scuff marks, all as part of a cue to concentrate on his responsibility. You have seen how planted distractions, such as a practical tracking dog will encounter, can be used to focus him more strongly on his job.

But possibly you might feel that much time has been spent on this foundation, and have heard of trainers who progressed much faster by using their own tracks to start their dogs, sometimes even retracing their steps so the dogs would have a "heavier scent" to follow. You might ask: "Why not use such a convenience?"

Think about it for a moment. If a handler lays a track for his own dog, and returns by the same route, thinking he'll make the track "heavier," he'll be asking the dog to run the track the wrong way. Obviously, the return track will be fresher, a fact that the dog will be asked to ignore as he's actually being ordered to backtrack.

One of a good tracker's greatest abilities is to recognize by minute variations indications of which way a track goes. A hunting hound that would run a track the wrong way, except when puzzling it out, would be disposed of as useless. So unless you are doing a "seek-back," don't encourage your dog to go against his instincts and common sense.

Later, for variety and to add a bit of zest, you can have him track you, but have another person handle him.

The reliability the good foundation has instilled in your dog on the short tracks should prepare you to handle any problems you might encounter as you begin the next level of training.

LEVEL 5

Objective: 100-foot track into the wind in harness.

Until now you've used short tracks in areas where it was easy to follow your dog, and the harness was on the dog merely as a part of a cue that it was time to track. All handling and correcting was done with your leash and collar. Now that your dog will be working longer tracks, it's time to use the harness and line. But leave the collar on in case the need for a correction should occur. If he is wearing a tab such as shown, you'll have a good handle to grab at such times.

You'll need an understanding of how you'll handle the line before you use it. A good precept would be, "with judicious restraint and without discouragement." Obviously, the actual mechanics of handling the line will be somewhat influenced by the terrain and vegetation where the track lies. But for some time your training courses will permit the dog to work about 10 feet in front of you, which would give him enough spectrum to make reasonable casts, and still place you close enough to observe and handle efficiently during these early training stages.

The best way to gauge the distance between yourself and the dog is to tie a knot in the line about 10 feet back from the snap. Let him go ahead of you until you feel the knot slide into your hand that feeds and handles the line, then apply some resistance. The dog thus

Now that your dog is working longer tracks, it's time to use the harness and line, but for awhile you might leave the collar and tab on, as shown, in case you need a "handle" for correction.

There should be some tension in the line so you can read your dog, but no discouragement. Make sure it doesn't catch in the brush or rocks and jerk your dog to a stop.

restricted will favor the ground scent, not cast wildly about scouting air-scent, nor scamper around to make visual checks, as is often done by the dog that plays a "game" on a line that is always slack. As to the goody-goody-gumdrop philosophy that restraint will confuse or discourage a dog, such drivel comes from that bottomless well of misinformation—the emotionalists who are unaware that there are motivations stronger than the games with which they insult a good dog's intelligence. A dog motivated by positive retrieving will not be discouraged by a moderately taut line, but will regard that bit of restraint as another reason to concentrate on his responsibility. When he pauses on the track, and the line slackens, you'll know that there are scent problems that he must solve before continuing on the track.

The above facts are some of the reasons why your dog should work on a snug line.

There are other reasons why the dog should work against restraint. Study the lower photo on the facing page. A line with tension will not foul on low brush nor rocks, which will be important when you progress to the level of practical tracking. But remember, there is a difference between a cooperative restraint and a solid jerk that could come if part of the line were to drop behind you and snag on something. Use one hand to prevent such accidental jerks. Your dog's ability, your own experience in handling, and the environmental conditions will determine the good average distances to work your dog. Awareness and practice will develop your skill in handling the line so it doesn't snag on objects nor entangle your dog.

Start the first period of this level by staking out a track about 60 feet long with a flag at the start and one at the finish. When the flags have been set, instruct the tracklayer to drop a sock about 20 feet out on the track, a second in another 20 feet, and a third at the end of the track, from where he will leave crosswind.

Let the body scent blow away from the track for a half-hour before you start to work it.

The close spacing of articles on a track is in accord with a policy that you should follow during the early stages of using positive retrieving as a motivation. Avoid "goofing gaps." Keep your dog aware that articles might occur in any number and at any time on a track and it is his responsibility to find them. Not only will this responsibility make it probable that he will find any evidence dropped on the tracks he works, it will keep him more closely oriented to the beam of ground scent that so unfailingly leads him to those objects.

Set up and work two more 60-foot tracks with him on this first day.

Second Through Fifth Days:

Extend the tracks 10 feet each day for four days. Use four socks dropped in approximately the same pattern as used previously. Work three tracks on each of the four days, or longer if needed to reach the point where your dog is tracking reliably into the wind for about 100 feet. Be certain you've reached that objective before you attempt Level Six.

LEVEL 6

Objective: To track across wind and downwind.

Until now any wind, even the gentlest air movement, except for occasional changes, brought the ground scent and residual body scent toward the dog, making it easy to follow the short, fresh tracks. Possibly you've been wondering how your dog will handle tracks that turn across the wind, and even downwind. Before we ask your dog to work out the turns, we'll give him experience in starting and following many short tracks laid in various relationships to the wind, so he can adjust to air movement that hampers rather than helps. The first few levels of instruction told you how to start and motivate a dog on short tracks that led him into the wind, beginning with the sight of the tracklayer so he would associate the air and ground scents, and the articles, with the man's person. Now we'll retrace those patterns in each detail, except for the way the tracks relate to the wind.

On the first day the tracks will be laid so the wind will move across it from the dog's right side. On the second day the tracks should lie so the air movement is against the dog's left side. On the third day the tracks should run downwind, blowing the scent directly away from the dog.

Remember, except for wind direction, you will apply the instructions for laying a track and handling your dog exactly as you did on the 30-foot tracks that led into the wind.

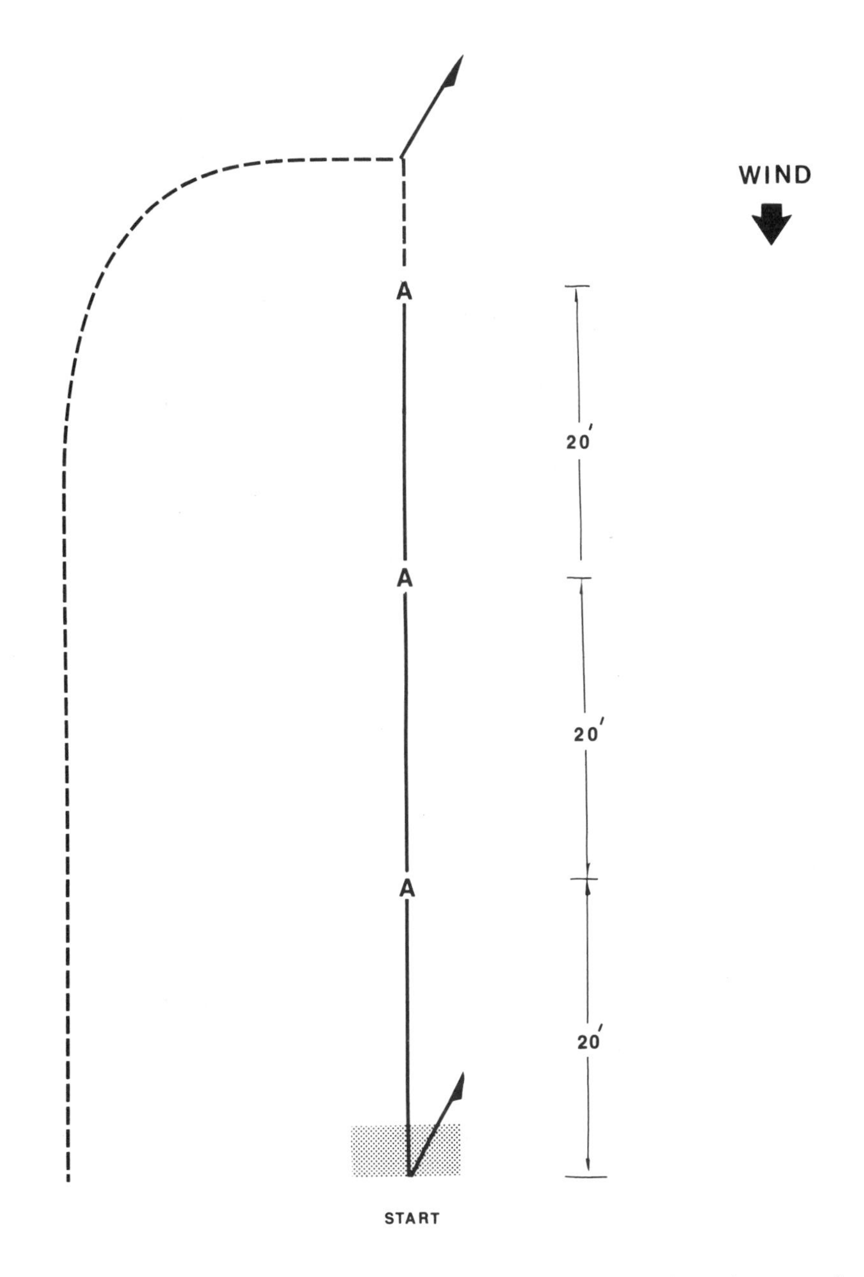

As you start to work longer tracks, it's good to use several articles spaced approximately as shown in the drawing.

You might be asking: "Why should the tracklayer be in sight on these 30-foot tracks when my dog has been solid on the 100-foot upwind tracks without the person's presence?"

Simple enough. *Sight of the man standing on the crosswind track will show your dog that there will be tracks that do not supply an airborne beam of body scent from the person, close though he might be.* But there will be ground scent from the tracks. And that ground scent will lead him to the objects he must find.

You should be able to introduce your dog to each of the new wind directions within a day, from the 30-foot tracks with the tracklayer in sight, through the 50-foot tracks that have aged a half hour and where the tracklayer is not in sight. You will be using six tracks a day, just as you did at the level where you started your dog into the wind. But watch your dog carefully. He'll tell you whether you need more work on any of the wind directions. If, whenever the wind does not bring the scent to him, he tracks with his nose close to the ground, you'll know he's ready for the next level.

LEVEL 7

Objective: Introduction to Turns.

You made the job of introducing turns easy when you showed your dog that tracks don't always run into the wind, and gave him experience in working out various wind components. On the first track of this level you are prepared to start the dog on a crosswind leg and make his first turn into the wind, which will be a very logical way to reward his ability and persistence.

Place a flag where you want your tracklayer to start a track that will run crosswind for about 50 feet with the air moving against his right side. He should scuff up a space to the right of the flag. The short crosswind leg is ample because your purpose is to provide experience on turns, not to practice straight tracks.

The tracklayer should drop a sock about 20 feet from the start and a knotted marking sock some 5 feet before he turns right and walks directly into the wind. About 15 feet after he's made the turn, he'll drop another sock for the dog to find and thus taste success for working out the problem. When the upwind leg is about 50 feet long, another marking sock should be dropped. This ends the track. The tracklayer should leave the spot by turning crosswind to his left and walking straight away far enough to prevent his residual scent from

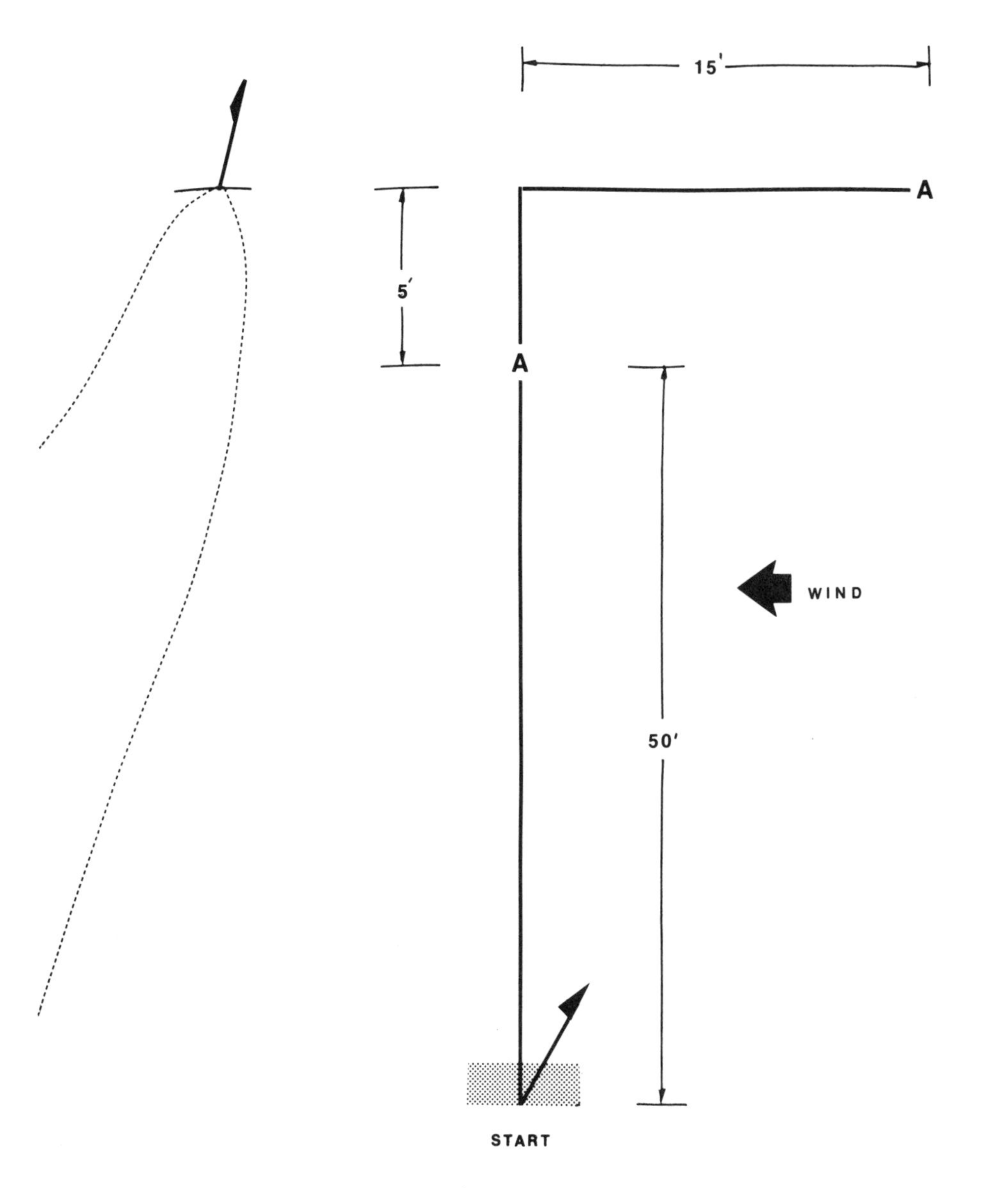

Introduction to the first turn. The drawing indicates approximate dimensions and directions in relation to the wind. Corners will often be more rounded.

blowing back across the first leg of the course. He should then clear out of the dog's line of vision.

Let the track age only about fifteen minutes before you start your dog. Such a short wait will make it probable that the direction of the wind will be the same as when the track was laid. If there is a drastic wind change, don't start. Wait a few minutes to see if the wind switches back to its previous direction, or, if the change seems fixed, plot another track.

Start and handle the dog as you usually do until he finds the marking sock which was dropped 5 feet before the turn, then supply enough resistance to slow him almost to a stop by the time he reaches the corner. Let just enough slack out so you can stop him if he goes 10 feet past the turn and while you are 5 feet back of the turning point so you will not be standing on ground that he has to recheck. Because the wind will be moving the scent from the new leg into him when he reaches the turn, he'll probably work the problem out easily and promptly. However, he might cast a few feet past the turn before he's convinced that the first leg has ended, so read him carefully. Again, do not let him go more than 10 feet past the turn before you stop him. Don't gesture, or in other ways try to show him the track turned. Let him work it out. Your restraint and his responsibility will cause him to work all of the scent that's available to him. When he works back toward you, he's bound to cross the scent coming off the upwind leg. Even if he's casting about in a pattern that brings him across the new leg upwind from the corner, the limited length of line should prevent him from hitting the track upwind of the sock. But if you do miscalculate the length of the line and he hits the new leg above the sock, go with him. It would be a mistake to stop his honest progress and bring him back to the sock.

If, instead of working the track out in the above ways, the dog gives up or simply goldbricks, grab the tab on his collar and correct him all the way to the sock. Don't let him con you with a quick burst of ambition in order to avoid the correction. Surely a dog that could follow the crosswind track is capable of working out a turn into the wind. If you don't let him goldbrick on the easy turns where the tracks are short and simple, you'll be able to trust his ambition and ability when the tracks are more difficult.

You've built a good foundation and the chances are good that

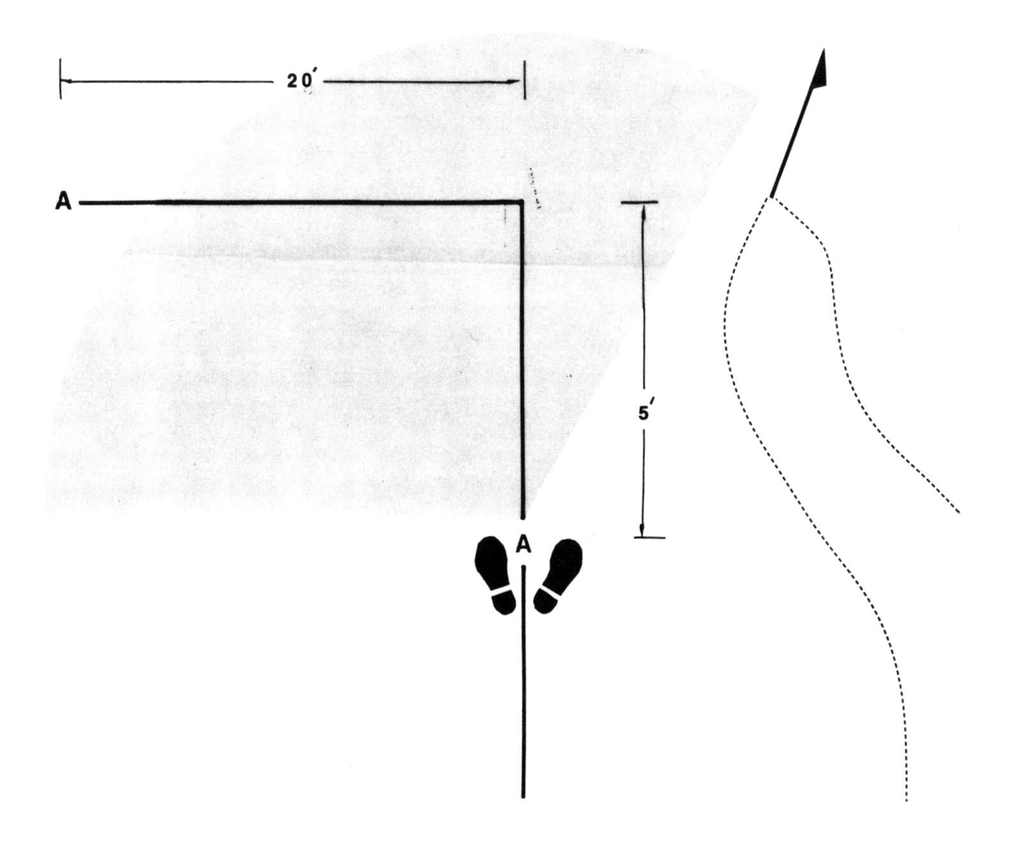

Give your dog an opportunity to work out the turn. Stop when you take the article from him and let him cast for the track in a pattern such as shown by the shaded area in the drawing.

he'll find it easy to follow the track from start to finish and find all the socks on the way.

Work him on three such patterns on the first day of this level.

Second Day:

The track should be laid and the socks placed the same as for the first turn except for one factor. The crosswind leg will be laid so the wind is blowing against the dog's left side until he makes the upwind turn. Work him on three of these left turn patterns during this second day.

Third Day:

All details of the above "experience pattern" will apply except for the direction of the first leg which will be into the wind, and the turn will be crosswind to the right. Remember, the first leg into the wind will be easy, and it is where the wind borne scent ends and the crosswind leg begins that a bit of difficulty could occur; and could require thoughtful and effective handling. Again, one day's work on each of three separate tracks should show him that tracks can turn in various directions.

Fourth Day:

Make only one change in the pattern. Lay the first leg into the wind but make a turn crosswind to the left. Work three of the patterns.

Fifth Day:

The first leg will be crosswind with the air movement against the dog's right side. The turn will be downwind so the track's scent will be carried away from the dog, making it necessary for him to work close to the ground and a bit slower than when the wind is helpful. Work three such tracks, or more if he has difficulty with the downwind turns.

Sixth Day:

The first leg will be crosswind with the wind moving against the dog's left side. Again, the turn will be downwind. Once more the track's scent will be carried directly away from him after the turn and he could experience a bit of difficulty, so give him a bit extra experience if you feel the need.

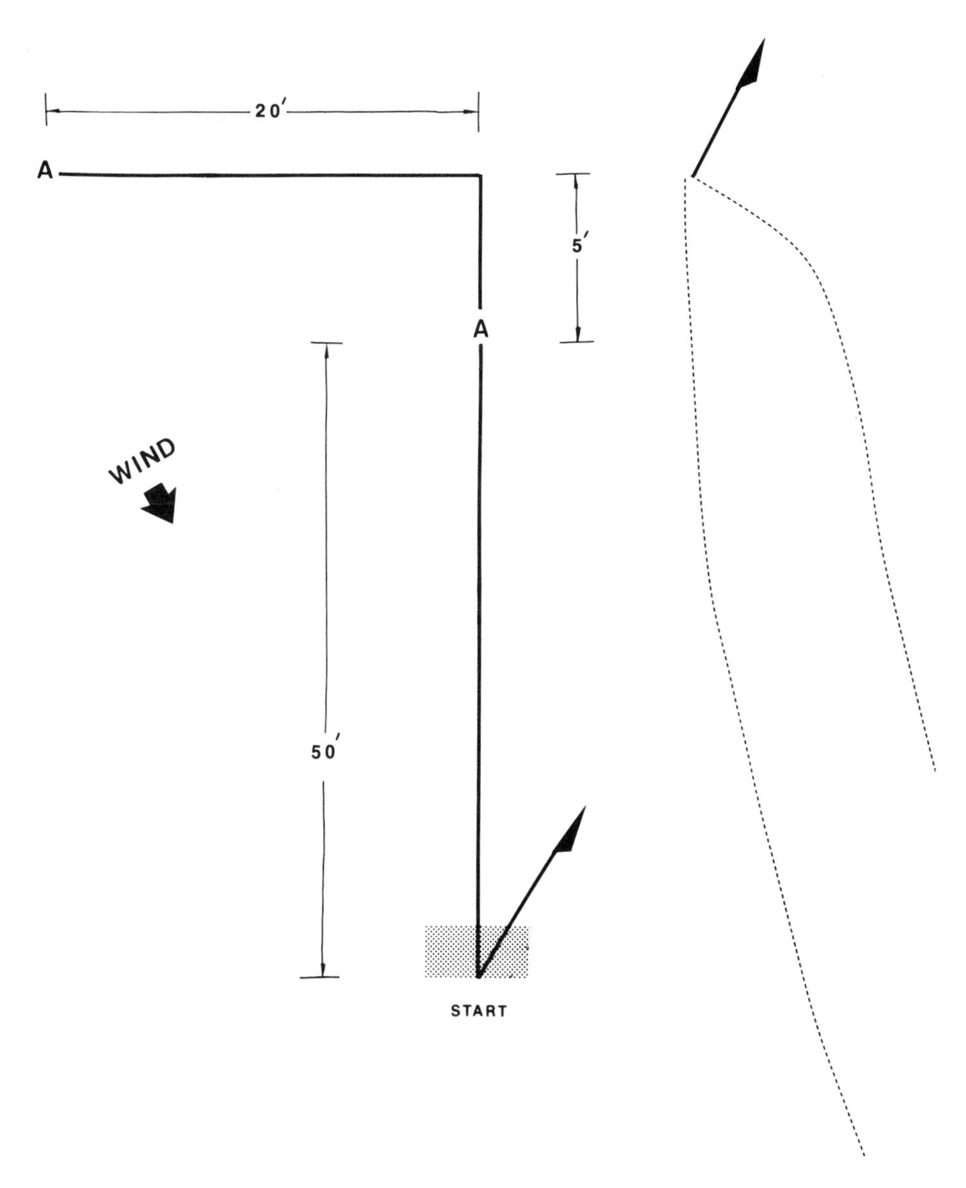

Practice turns in varied relationship to the wind, including quartering winds as shown in the drawing.

Seventh Day:

The first leg should be laid downwind, and the turn should be made crosswind to the left. Work three such tracks.

Eighth Day:

The first leg should be laid downwind, and the turn should be made crosswind to the right. Work three such tracks.

From your own observations you will decide on the wind directions and turns that seem to be the most difficult for your dog to handle, and plot tracks to give your dog the experience he needs. For reasons known only to dogs, some directions and conditions seem to pose difficulties that we humans do not understand.

Use line drawings to describe how a variety of sample tracks relate to different wind conditions, and note the harmfulness of possibly misreading those relationships.

It is the author's belief that, if you enter such a study creatively by conceiving and drawing some of your own diagrams, you will become more aware of the wind's relationship to the tracks and your dog than if you merely viewed another's drawing. To lay extensive tracks without a complete awareness of wind relationship to all parts of the tracks could cause you to misunderstand why your dog leaves a track to go to a scent that is blown from a fresher leg of the track that was thoughtlessly laid so that its scent drifts back across the previous leg.

From the background of your own thoughts on what would be unfair to a dog in training, study the wind and discuss the facts with your tracklayer as you plot each track.

You've given your dog experience on short, straight tracks that ran into the wind, and on turns that combined a wide variety of directions. Because you worked in carefully structured, logical progressions you were able to correct and praise in a meaningful way. You've demonstrated your mastery of enough situations to convince him there's no way he can con you. Satisfying experience has awakened all his inherent ability to track and now he's really enjoying his work. The fact that his own pleasure in tracking is undergirded by his respect for your authority has increased that pleasure and made him wonderfully reliable. The above status qualifies you and your dog to begin work on longer and more complex tracks.

Extend the straight tracks progressively each day for weekly increases of about 100 feet. Let the tracks age a bit more each time as your dog's ability develops. For a couple of months work in areas that you feel offer reasonably good conditions for your dog to track and you to handle him. Add turns so he'll gain experience in working out wind changes before you start on problems such as described in the practical tracking section of this book.

Your tracklayer should have enough socks so he can drop one on the track about 10 yards from the starting point, and one about 5 feet before each turn, one 20 feet after each turn, and one at the track's end.

By the time you have used the principles and schedules set forth to this point, results will show you that your dog's work doesn't depend on bribery or his natural inclinations at a particular moment. You might feel you could motivate your dog to track under all reasonable conditions. But you'll need more than that good foundation and confidence. You'll need to understand the physical conditions that relate to a track and to be keenly aware of them as you increase the lengths of the tracks and vary your work areas.

Any skilled handler of military scout dogs will tell you that surface winds can vary in stratas that are a few feet in depth. Contours and vegetation can cause splits and deviations in air movement that would shock anyone who sees the effect of wind in trees and supposes that the currents must be the same at ground levels.

The key to wind-awareness is not to memorize a lot of gerrymandering line drawings that picture scent direction relative to the track and the course a dog must travel to find or follow the scent. Those lines won't be out in the field to help you appreciate a problem that your dog might encounter. But there's something that will always be with you. It's your ability to read your dog's performance relative to the air movement that careful checking shows you exists at ground level. Your experience in reading your dog in the carefully structured progressions, plus concentration, should have given you that essential to good handling.

Work thoughtfully as you increase the length of the tracks and the time they have aged, and vary the kinds of areas where your dog tracks. You and your dog should work reliably on tracks 1500 feet long that have aged 2 hours before you use the next section of this book.

Much time can be saved in a tracking class by having the members lay their tracks simultaneously.

When the waiting period is over, all the dogs can be started on their assigned tracks at the same time.

3

Preparing for the T.D. Test

IT'S A FACT that participants in most learning programs do their best when they have definite targets and carefully structured steps to lead them to their goals. Whether or not you wish to obtain tracking titles, sample tracks for the T.D. and T.D.X. tests will furnish useful targets and practice in your program to develop a practical tracking dog. Furthermore, it is hoped that your success with those tracks will encourage you to enjoy the fun of acquiring at least a "T."

An overview of how tracking trials are regulated and staged is the logical place to begin the above work. Such familiarizing will not in itself make you more competent but, as it defines some training objectives, will make you more confident. Carefully study the AKC Regulations and the description of an acceptable track.

Unlike the Obedience Trials where conditions and dimensions are closely standardized, tracks and conditions will vary from one area to another. Regulations will allow for variation as to where turns will be located and the kinds of terrain that will be used. Such factors as wind velocity and direction and the humidity will vary from one part of a track to another, and can change dramatically within minutes. Because of the uncontrollable aspects of the sport, there is less griping about "bad judging and poor conditions" than in other dog sports.

Rarely in a Tracking Test will the "breaks" be even from one track to another or from one hour to another. Don't merely hope for favorable conditions. Prepare for the worst. Then hope for the best.

If you have followed the instructions given in this book thus far, you and your dog should be qualified to start practice on typical T.D. tracks. Actually, the practice tracks we'll use will be a bit more difficult than those laid for a Test, because we'll require your dog to find a number of objects on the track, in addition to the object at the end of the course. Our procedure will give you the opportunity to detect and logically correct irresponsible work instead of practicing mistakes.

You can have someone pre-stake a track for your tracklayer a day before he lays it, as is done for an Official Test, or you can use a sketch and verbal explanation to describe a pattern he can use. But in either case, a starting flag and a 30-yard flag should be used in practice just as they are in a Test, and they should not be set by the tracklayer. On any course that was prestaked, the tracklayer will collect all but the first two flags as he lays the track, unless your basic work was inadequate and you still need flags for further training. But bear in mind, if you do need any indications of turns or direction, that the tracklayer can drop articles of a kind that would give you such information as well as a flag would. A sock with two knots can mean "left turn," as well as be something handy for your dog to find and you to carry. Work out a simple code with your tracklayer.

As has been said before, changes in the wind will sometimes occur between the time a track is laid and when it is worked, but try to use a variety of wind problems. Work closely with your tracklayer on what you want to accomplish, collaborating on simple line drawings. It's best to do this just before he lays the track so he can relate the features of the track he lays to the wind conditions at the time.

Your tracklayer will need to pre-scent six articles, one of which must be a leather glove or another acceptable article such as the one that must be dropped at the end of an official Track. He should scuff up a scent bed beside the flag that is set to mark the start of a track, walk straight toward the 30 yard flag and drop a sock on the track about 20 feet from where he started. Approximately 70 yards after he passes the flag he should drop a knotted sock or another marker

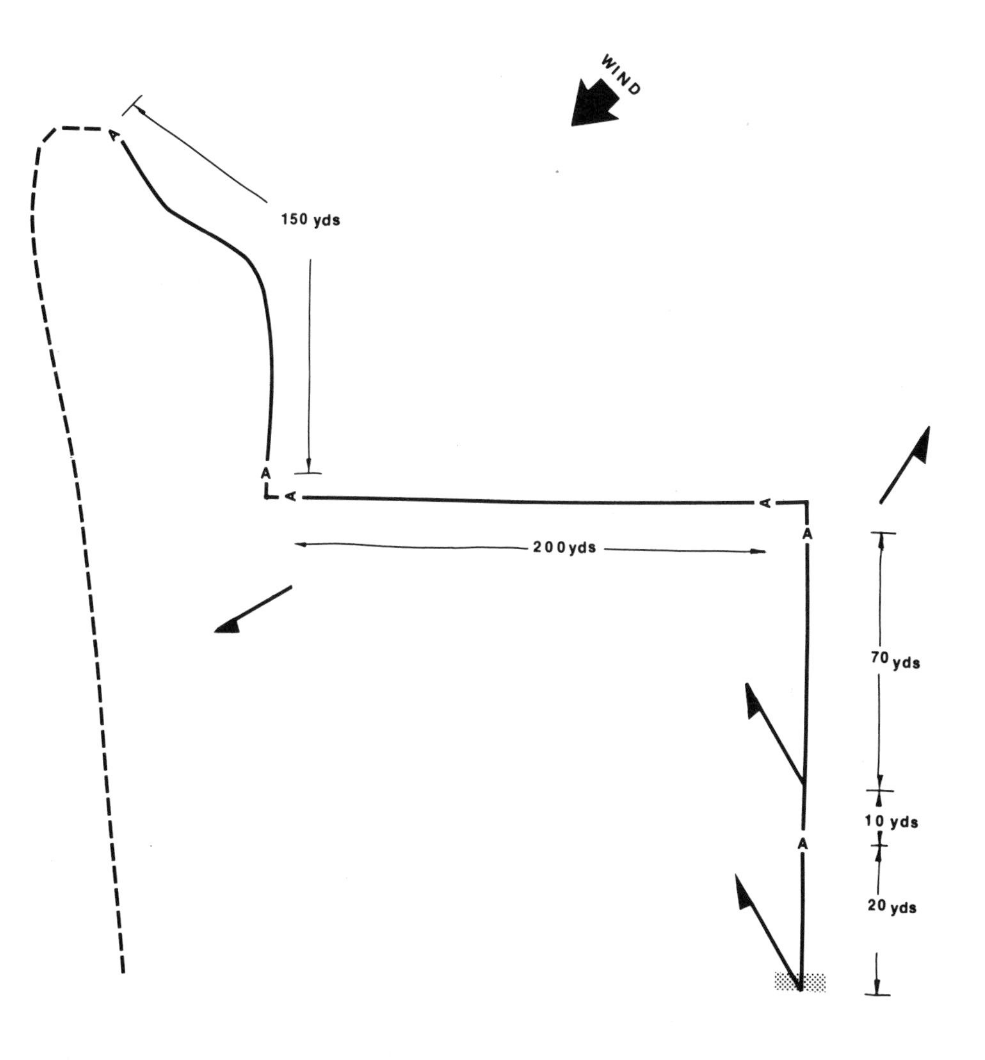

Wind relationship to a track that runs in various directions is hard to anticipate, but the arrow will show an attempt to keep the wind from blowing the scent from one leg back onto another.

to indicate the track will turn left after another ten steps. Ten steps after he makes the turn, he will drop another sock for your dog to find and feel rewarded.

Approximately 200 yards farther on, he should drop a sock and turn right after ten steps. As before, he will drop another sock ten steps after he makes the turn so your dog will have another opportunity for success and praise, and so you will be able to make a meaningful correction, in the unlikely case it is needed. After he makes the right turn the tracklayer should walk a casually meandering course for about another 150 yards, being careful not to go directly upwind of any previous part of the track, which could cause the dog to work any late drifting body scent instead of sticking to the track.

He will drop the "official leather article" at the end of the track, then exit the track pattern by a route that will keep his body scent from drifting over any part of the course.

Always heel your dog to within a few feet of the starting mark before you put the harness on him.

When you start him, pay close attention to how he's working under the prevailing conditions. The flags will show you how the wind relates to the alignment of the track.

Wait an hour before you start your dog. Bring him close to the trackhead and equip him with the harness and line as part of the pattern you will follow even in a Test. As usual, have him hold a down with his nose over the scent bed to memorize the track's scent. Occasionally, a dog's competence and eagerness will cause an over-confident handler to change or skip a part of the significant pattern that focuses a dog on his responsibility, before advanced training has substituted some other cues. Such carelessness can give a dog a bad break in a Test because it starts him before he's really plugged into the scent.

After the "memorizing period," start him. Pay close attention to how he's working under the prevailing conditions. The flags will definitely show you the alignment of the track and give some indication of how the wind relates to it. Remember, you will have two such flags when you work in a trial, so pay close attention as to how he handles the first 30 yards of the course. This will help you to know what to expect under the conditions that exist.

In your basic training you started tracks that were laid in all significant relationships to the wind, so regardless of how the wind relates to the starting leg of your sample Test Tracks, your dog should have little difficulty in starting and following the track regardless of how it relates to air movement.

Although there will only be one article for your dog to find in a

Test, his responsibility to find an unknown number, and sustained concentration will remind you of the value of using multiple articles in practice. But there is another reason to keep the dog responsible for finding a number of articles that bear the tracklayer's scent. It will be emphasized later when we deal with the value of finding evidence on a track.

As always, praise him a lot when he finds the article before and after the turns, and have a celebration when he finds that "official article" at the end of the track. But don't turn him loose to celebrate hysterically in the tracking area. Replace the harness and longe with your collar and leash and take him from the field at heel. Postpone any breaks and relief stops until you are out of the tracking environment.

Your basic training and practice have taught you how to deal with any problems that might occur on your sample Test Tracks, so your handling from the start to the article at the end should be mostly routine.

However, if you should experience any unusual difficulties that seem peculiar to the situation, Chapter 8—which deals with a variety of problems—could be helpful to you.

Probably your dog will work a track such as the above quite easily, but it would be foolish to try for your "T" without more practice. Work on two or three such tracks a week, each about 500 yards, which is longer than most of those laid for a Test. Increase the aging period progressively until you're working tracks at least two hours old, which is the maximum time required for a "T". Vary the conditions of wind and terrain when you practice. *Don't consider having your dog certified until you feel comfortable running practice tracks such as above.*

One of the things that sets competition apart from practice is the need to focus the dog immediately and intently on a job or exercise without any excuses or false starts. Lack of this essential generally comes from mistakes that are made by apologetic, nervous handlers when practicing. You have probably seen such inadequacy demonstrated at all levels of obedience. For example, a mentally infirm handler working on such a simple exercise as the heel-free will sometimes give double commands, coax, pat a leg, or do other things to try to get his dog to perform correctly, instead of working intelligently to correct the fault. When these excessive cues cause the dog to adjust temporarily to a better position, the handler feels he has actually accomplished something. Then when he enters competition, regulations prevent him from giving any second commands or cues and the dog realizes that different conditions prevail; and his training had developed no sense of responsibility to keep him honest in those moments when extra cues are forbidden. In tracking with a well prepared dog, there is no reason to handle differently in a test than in practice, but sometimes a handler will choke up a bit when he sees the "official looking" environment of lots of dogs and hears pre-trial apologies of nervous handlers who are scrutinizing the physical situation for reasons to later justify their dogs' failures, or are recalling the number of times failures resulted from such unfavorable conditions.

Practice the foregoing variety of sample tracks until you feel that you and your dog are prepared to work them under all kinds of conditions. Then it will be time to have your dog certified for participation in a Tracking Test. Regulations allow any AKC approved tracking judge to certify a dog. Because you are interested in tracking, you are probably aware of the closest available judge. Unless the one you contact lives close to where a track can be laid, it might be most convenient for him to come to your training area and direct the laying of what he considers an acceptable test track.

Before you work your dog in competition, make it a point to visit a Tracking Test with your dog. When you reach the trial grounds, be sure to park in an approved place, and leave him in the car while you locate the designated relief area, so what appears to be unused space is not the location of part of a track. Although your dog will not be tracking, you can begin to let him know that a tracking trial is an environment where you expect him to act responsibly. Have him at heel when you take him from the car to the relief area, and demand that he heel correctly regardless of the strange people and dogs around him. Give him your word of release to relax and relieve himself; then bring him under command again as you mingle with the spectators to watch the proceedings. Convince him that this is an environment where he should ignore the other dogs and their handlers even if they make friendly advances to him.

Your training and practice with the tracking dog has shown you that the activity does not feature the precision one sees in the obedience ring where all moves are made to a predictable and exact

Practice on wet as well as dry surfaces.

A track laid through a busy park can provide some good practice.

standard; but you notice that a number of handlers have leaned so far the other way in their attitude that they've convinced their dogs that this is a frivolous affair and not to be taken seriously. They laugh when several of the more animated dogs try to promote a play session; and no obedience commands are enforced.

There is evidence that the "fun and games" that some of the dogs showed during the waiting period continues to dominate when they are called upon to start their tracks. Some of them are more interested in the quail-like flights of meadow larks. Other dogs are given only a brief sniff at the track-head by nervous handlers before they are started, then move out high-headed as though wondering what they should do. Somehow as you watch a number of dogs make their way across the field obviously intrigued with the myriad of sights and scents, it becomes easy for you to understand why the ratio of success among "T" candidates is only a bit above one in ten in most Tracking Tests. Watch carefully so you'll profit from what you see.

THE LAST WEEK

You have worked with your dog on tracks that should have prepared the two of you for any challenges you might meet in a T.D. Test. You have studied the regulations and have visited at least one Tracking Test to observe the environment and demands, and have practiced thoughtfully to prepare for them. Your dog worked well in his certification test, and so you made your entry. The day of the Test is drawing close and you're wondering if there are any final thoughts that might be helpful. Certainly, there are a few bits of common sense that can help your dog put his best nose forward.

If your locale is cooking during a hot and dry spell, try to work your practice tracks in an area that's free of weed seeds and excessive dust. This is not because such things can make a track difficult; they can start a mechanical irritation that might be in full bloom on the big day. Under normal conditions, there is no reason why your dog shouldn't run your usual schedule of practice tracks prior to the Test; but let him rest at least two days before the event so he'll be charged up physically and mentally by the time you put him down on that first Official Track. Also, this will lessen any chance of his snuffing up any dust or seeds just before he needs his nose the most.

Be sure to have all the things you'll need for the test ready so there'll be no last minute panic search. This list should include more than the harness, line, and acceptable article. For your dog's comfort take a pan and a jug of water, a leather collar and a chain so you can give him a quiet break instead of a wild, sustained celebration when you get that "T". You might want to compete again and it's best that he remember a Test environment as a place where he should be calm, not hysterical. Probably you'll have a bit of a drive to the trial site; start early so there'll be time to get a good parking place and to be able to let your dog relieve himself and become comfortable. Check in with the officials as soon as you arrive so they'll know you're at hand when they draw for track assignments. By paying attention to the above details you will be able to relax and let your composure tell your dog that there is really nothing unusual about the environment and all systems are go.

Don't be depressed if other dogs work before yours and you see them have trouble. Your dog will be running his own track and different conditions are apt to prevail when he works. And it is quite probable that any failures you see will be due to lack of a realistic motivation rather than to real difficulties.

Allow sufficient time before your dog will track to exercise him a bit. Don't change any of the preliminaries you used in practice to tell him it's time to go to work. Put the harness on him and attach the line in the usual relation to the place and time of starting, and, when you down him on the scent mark give some thought to the wind conditions so his nose is in the best spot to catch the scent. Don't let the fact that the judges are waiting, nor nervousness, cause you to start your dog sooner or any different than you would in practice.

Between the time he starts and reaches the 30 yard flag, you will be able to tell somewhat how he can perform under the conditions that exist. You'll be more comfortable and be able to do your best job of handling if you know how he is affected by the track conditions that prevail. Keep the same amount of tension in the line as you do in practice, and in other ways try to express your usual confidence. Although he needs only to locate the article that marks the track's end, give him a chance to pick it up for you before you hold it high in victory.

Congratulations!

4

Preparing for the T.D.X. Test

IT SOMETIMES comes as a surprise to those who have had no experience with hunting hounds or other field dogs to learn of the miles of rough ground such dogs will cover on a single hunt. When they compare such performances with the 1000 yards of a T.D.X. Track that is laid on comparatively smooth ground, they are convinced that the formal tracking test is not much of a physical challenge. But there are some factors that can make the longer T.D.X. tracks more difficult than those required in the T.D. Test. Under some conditions, the added time of exposure on the longer tracks can cause a busy nose to load with dust and seeds, which can make a dog's job harder. The effect of mechanical factors is often seen in spaniels when they're hunting dusty cover. Dust will absorb the moisture in the nose to a point where mud is actually created in the nostrils. You won't be able to do anything about the conditions where your dog will be tested, but you can certainly make his job easier if you have him in top condition. In addition to promoting his general good health, supplementary minerals and vitamins can help to keep his sensing areas and respiratory system healthy in the face of rough conditions. Be alert to any snuffing or sneezing that might be caused by an obstruction such as a foxtail or other weed. Depend on your veterinarian's skill and equipment to quickly check for such difficulties if your dog sniffles or sneezes for any length of time.

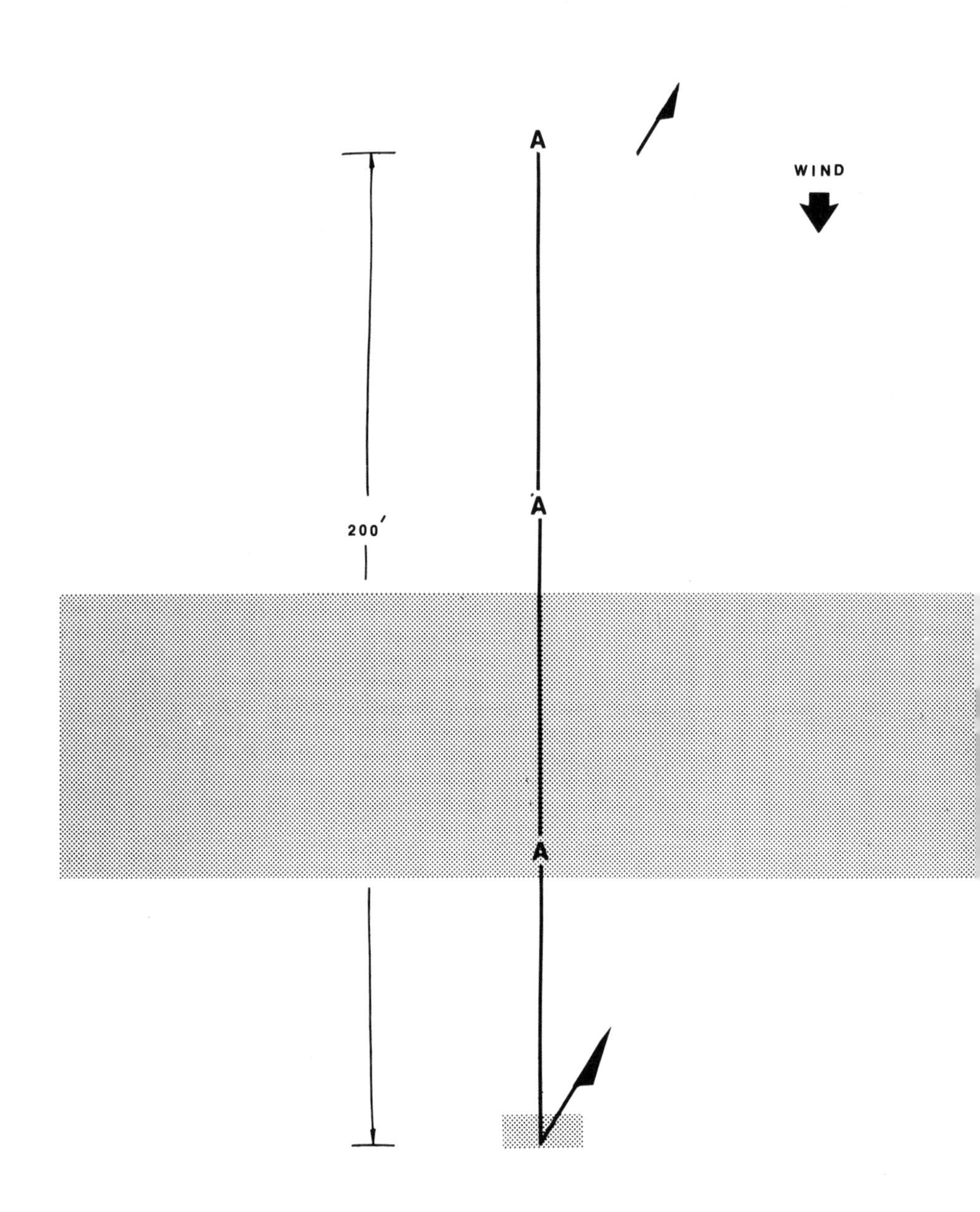

Study the text carefully. It can make the job of tracking across pavements easy for you.

The mental and physical conditioning that gives an edge in any kind of a test generally comes from training experience that demands more than will be needed in the actual event. This means you will have to observe carefully and train thoughtfully. The following suggestions should help you to prepare for a hard test in a way that will permit you to accurately observe his performance on each of the training components.

Begin by increasing the track length 50 feet each day beyond the distances you practiced for the T.D. Tests. Do not include any turns, cross tracks, or road crossings while you work to increase his endurance. We want him to enjoy continued success as the tracks grow longer. We'll work on the track complications separately so his learning experience will be the fullest and you can read him the most accurately. Use five or six articles on your long tracks, spaced at random, and have your helper drop a leather object where he ends the track. Two of these long tracks each week is a reasonable number for the average dog. As said before, make your own careful observations of how your dog handles these long, but uncomplicated tracks.

During other periods that are separated by at least an hour from the time you work on the long tracks you can work on the complications that are part of the T.D.X. Test. Regulations require several kinds of challenges to be used. Let's start with "lightly traveled roads."

Find an area where your tracklayer can lay a track about 200 feet long that crosses a sidewalk or narrow pavement, either concrete or macadam. We will drop an article a couple of steps out on the pavement, another a few feet past the pavement, and a third to indicate the track's end, and to let the dog feel a second success for tracking across the pavement. The track's relation to the wind will not be important to your dog at this point, but, as always, the tracklayer should leave the area in a way that keeps his scent from blowing back toward the track.

The fact that many trainers fail to practice tracking on pavement has caused quite a number of dogs to regard such surfaces as reservations where tracks are never followed. Such a mental block has caused the misconception that dogs find it tremendously difficult to track on paved surfaces. You might find that your dog can do very well on many supposedly difficult surfaces if you practice on them to let him know that tracks are not limited to earth and vegetation.

Let the track age for about half an hour before you start your dog. As planned, the track to the pavement will be easy for him to follow. It's when he reaches the edge of the pavement that you might notice a change in his performance. As said before, do not believe that any hesitancy to follow the track onto the road is due to inability to track on such a surface. If he stops when he reaches the pavement, don't waste his time with explanations about paving materials. Correct him right to the article and see that he picks it up. Probably he will track to the article without the need for correction even though this is his first track on pavement, and you'll get the chance to pour the praise on him.

Start him out again on the remainder of the track, and give him a lot more praise when he works his way to the last article and picks it up.

Stay with the pattern of a short track that crosses a pavement, working a couple of patterns each day, and progressively using wider drives and roads until your dog shows you he knows that tracks don't always end at pavements, but often leave their scent on the hard surfaces and continue on the other side.

For the record, don't be surprised if you find your dog can often track rather easily across concrete and macadam.

If the age or poor conditions should make a track hard to puzzle out, he will still have learned to cross a pavement and cast for it on the far side.

Reviewing Turns:

You worked your dog on turns that ran in all directions to the wind when you did your basic training. Now when your dog seems to endure well on the long simple tracks, it will be time to include a number of those turns as you continue to work on endurance. T.D.X. tracks require "at least three right-angle turns and should include more than three such turns," but we'll use a greater number of turns in our practice. Also, for purposes of training and holding your dog to responsibility, we'll use a number of articles on the track. Have your tracklayer drop one of a variety of articles about six steps after every turn so your dog will be rewarded with a "find" and be encouraged to work purposefully.

Cross Tracks:

An hour after an official T.D.X. Track is laid, two strangers will lay tracks that cross the assigned track in two places. This is done to see whether a dog stays responsibly with the track he should follow or switches to a fresher cross track.

Some trainers would have you believe that when cross tracks are a lot fresher than the assigned track they are a strong diversion for a dog. Let's look at the situation logically. Is it not true that before he reaches a cross track a dog would have to follow the assigned track for considerable distance? Can you believe that, just as he reaches a cross track, a dog is struck with a mysterious inability to smell the track he has followed to that point? Or when it was bisected by the cross track did the main track instantly lose its distinctive scent? "No" is the obvious answer to all the above.

The reason for any diversion was not inability. More than likely it was flabby motivation. Bribes and games will awaken a dog's natural desire, but it will not undergird that desire with responsible behavior that is stronger than instinctive behavior. A positive motivation will awaken natural drives and also support them with a foundation of responsibility, because the dog has learned his actions must answer to more than inclinations. At the deepest level, nothing is more "natural" than necessity. It's a part of the universal order. So it's natural, when he works an assigned course to a cross track, to demand that he use his proven ability to discriminate between his responsibility and a diversion.

The chances are your purposeful dog will ignore a cross track, but a little diversion-proofing might give you added confidence.

Once again we will use the technique of bouncing a dog's attention off a planted distraction back to his responsibility so cross tracks become "taboo tracks." Because you have used the principle in earlier training, you'll immediately understand the process, but follow the instructions carefully.

Select an area with enough room for a main track about 300 feet long. You or someone older than the tracklayer should set a flag to guide your tracklayer and the one who lays the crosstrack. Your tracklayer should scuff a starting mark about 200 feet from the flag, and lay a track that will pass a couple of feet to one side of the flag stake. A few feet after he passes the flag, he should drop a sock, then

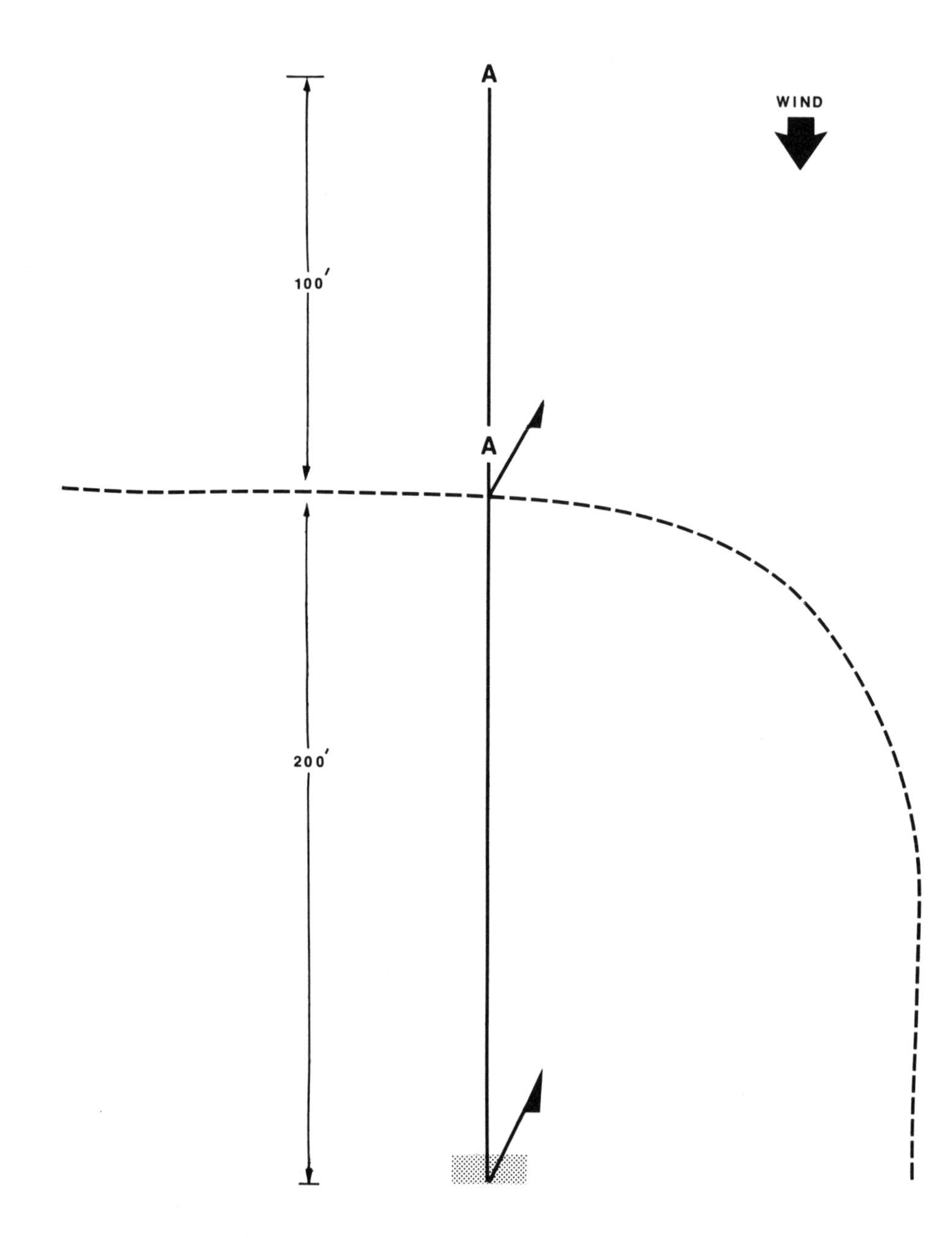

The solid line represents the main track and the broken line shows the "flavorful" crosstrack.

continue on for another hundred feet. He will drop another sock to end the track, and clear out of the area.

On an official T.D.X. Track, two persons walk close together across the assigned track, but we can start out with the track of one person. To help your dog suspect that cross tracks are taboo tracks, and are laid to divert him, we will make the first few of them redundantly tempting. Have the person who will lay the cross track rub a bacon rind or another savory substance on his soles.

An hour after the main track was laid, your "scented" cross tracklayer should approach it from a right angle at a latitude that will take him across the main track a foot from the flag. His cross track should continue about 50 feet past the main track, then he can leave the area without concern for any way in which scent from his track or body might be blown about. After all, your dog is being sacked off the tempting scent of cross tracks.

When the main track has aged two hours the cross track will be only an hour old and much fresher than the other, and it will be time to start your dog. As usual during training leave the collar and short tab on the dog when you equip him with the harness and line. Everything else about the start should be the same as usual. It will be about 200 feet to where the flag marks the cross track, and you'll be close behind him when he reaches the point of "decision." Be ready when he gets to the intersection. Probably your previous work on distractions will cause him to regard the fresher and flavorful cross track as a strong cue to concentrate on his responsibility and have his good judgment confirmed by picking up the sock and reaping tons of praise. After the celebration, start him out on the remainder of the track to get the last article.

If instead of tracking responsibility across the temptation, he succumbs to the fresher and more inviting track, give him a few seconds to correct his mistake, then, if he continues a wrong course, make a correction that snatches him back to the intersection and then along the track to the article.

The drawing on Page 72 will clearly show you the relationship of the main track and the cross track.

Praise him when he picks the article up, and pick it up he will if he's had realistic fundamental training.

As has been said before, if you have skillfully used distractions throughout your obedience training to teach your dog that

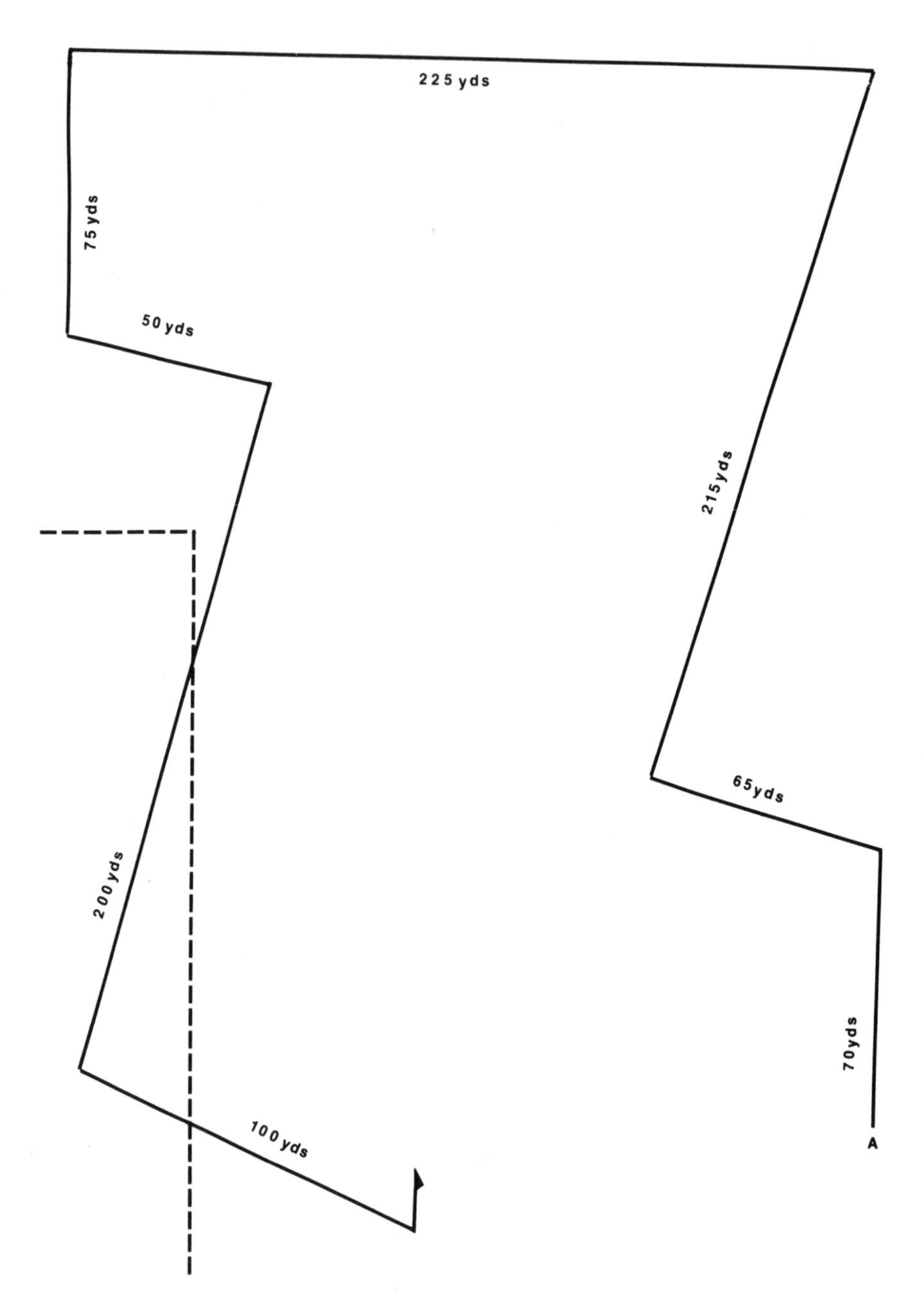

The broken line in this drawing shows how crosstracks can angle across the main track. You and your helpers can use the drawing to plan your own problems.

temptations are reasons to concentrate on his job, you should have little trouble with cross tracks. Continue to work in the above pattern, letting the tracks age a bit longer each day until the main track is three hours old. When you reach that point, let the cross track bear only the scent of two people who walk side by side across it, without the addition of any tempting scents on their soles. Also, at this time it will be advisable to lay several of such tracks across the main track, first planting the flags so they and the main tracklayer and you will know where the crossings will be set, and you will know where the articles lie and be prepared to act accordingly. Three of these cross tracks can be laid across a main track 300 feet long. Quite obviously, there need be no concern with the direction the cross tracks are laid in relation to the wind.

There will be days when scent conditions cause a fading that leaves the fresher cross track more discernible than the main track, but don't let your dog con you. *Remember, if the scent was sufficiently workable for the dog to start and follow the main track, there is no reason to believe it suddenly disappeared when he reached the cross track. It continued on ahead—and so should your dog. If conditions are difficult, you'll know it soon after you start him, before you get to the cross track.*

When your dog is taking the cross tracks that are laid in your short patterns, as cue to apply himself even more earnestly to his responsibility, you can arrange for cross tracks to intersect the long practice tracks you've been working. To know exactly where cross tracks are staged so you can act appropriately, be sure your tracklayer understands all details each time you set up the patterns.

Training even an inferior dog to the point where he rejects cross tracks is as simple as training dogs in an Open Obedience class to retrieve in close proximity to temptations when he has had a foundation of realistic basic training. But again be warned that if your dog was coaxed, baited and double commanded into routines that you mistook for obedience, there's a possibility that he might take the correction for goofing on a cross track as a reason to say, "I'll quit." And you, having previously proven yourself infirm, would probably say, "Oh Dear."

A trainer of average intelligence and ability should have little difficulty in using the foregoing principles and techniques to prepare his dog to handle the turns, road crossings and cross tracks that are part of a T.D.X. Test.

When you've reached that level of competence, it will make your success in competition more certain if you overextend a bit in practice. Lengthen your tracks to about twice the distance required in a test, and include three cross tracks, laid an hour later than the main tracks, two road crossings, and eight turns, some sharp and others more rounded. Gradually let the tracks age a bit longer until your dog is working tracks three hours old. Such extensive work is time consuming, but try to lay two tracks a week. If possible, vary the time of day and weather conditions for your practice.

A week before you work your dog in a Test, observe the same precautions that were recommended when you prepared for the T.D. Test.

5

A Test for Scouting

A YOUNG MOTHER took the handkerchief from her wet face and watched the deputy sheriff make notes on his pad. "We finished eating about two o'clock," she said. "Randy and the other kids started playing hide-and-seek on the edge of the woods. None of us realized how dense the underbrush is a short distance back in the timber. We thought he was just hiding until the kids gave up trying to find him. We all looked and looked. Now it's getting close to night."

The deputy looked at the dark fringe of growth that outlined the picnic area. "How long have you been looking?" he asked.

"At least three hours," she answered. "We've searched in every direction, listening and calling continually. There's no trace of him."

As the two talked, a group of children sat solemnly on the benches, supervised by one parent. The other parents, in the pattern of ants, came from the woods and then returned by the paths that others had just left.

"Do you think a dog could help find him?" Randy's mother asked.

"It's possible," the deputy said. "There's a local dog club that has a couple of dogs with tracking titles. We put in a request for one as soon as we got the call on your boy. The dog should be here soon."

The deputy's manner and tone seemed to force a confidence he didn't feel. His expression didn't change as he turned to where a

An accomplished tracking dog needs experience on the tracks of children. Kids choose routes through and under obstacles that adults avoid.

station wagon stopped in the parking area, and a middle-aged woman got out and opened the tailgate.

She fastened a leash to the collar of an alert German Shepherd Dog, took a tracking line and harness from a tack box and came over to the deputy. She listened attentively while he explained the situation.

"They've been trampling around in there for hours," she said. "But maybe there's one place where you know the boy walked and the others didn't foul the track. Then I can start the dog on one clean scent."

"Not that I know of," the deputy answered. "Would it help if we can get something of the boy's for him to smell?"

"Probably not," the woman said. "He's only trained to work tracks he's started on. I'll take him out so he can scout around for airborne scents, but he'll simply alert on the first person he senses."

The deputy watched as the frustrated searchers came out of the timber and stood talking, or sagged tiredly onto the picnic benches.

"They're giving up," he said. "I'll hold them all out of the woods so your dog will have a better chance."

"It will be a small chance," the dog handler said. "That's all a dog ever gets. A small chance."

The deputy nodded. "That's the way it is. They're always going to tramp around before they call for help."

The foregoing example of the chaos that explodes when a child is lost is generally duplicated at the scene of a crime where it could be important to learn as much as possible about a suspect's departure. The two kinds of situations have a common denominator. Each is an emergency. It is natural that those present at an emergency try to act quickly in order to solve a problem. When those first efforts fail, other procedures are started. Experts called can only hope that all significant evidence has not been obliterated. Experts that respond to a lost-person call generally arrive after volunteers have stomped the ground into an unreadable mess. It's laughable to expect a dog employed in such situations to be started as he would in a formal tracking trial. At best, lost kids and suspects do not make a mark nor post a flag for the handler and dog, nor start their tracks in a protected area.

Fortunately, a good handler with a practical tracking dog does

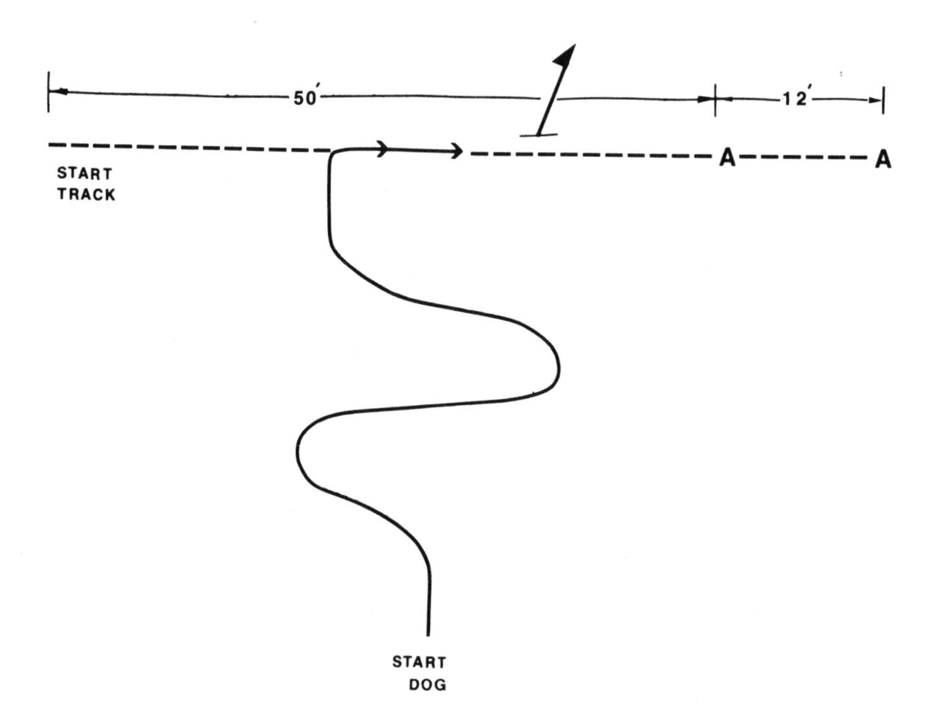

The wavering line shows how the pattern will take your dog to where the track lies and the wind helps. It's a rare dog that would find this test difficult.

not need to depend on the conventional ways to start a track. This book will present a realistic way to train and start a dog for emergency situations.

There is a test that will tell whether you and your dog are ready to begin the work explained in the next section of this book. If you have worked correctly and sufficiently, you will find the test quite simple. If you omitted some of the early work as unnecessary for your dog, or tried to hybridize the philosophy, you might decide to turn back and include some of the steps you neglected.

Now call to mind the most important things your dog acquired from his foundation work in tracking. Surely two of them should have been his responsibility to move out in response to your fetch-command, and the ability to solve turns and other problems by going close to the ground scent, knowing it was a beam that could take him to something he should retrieve. Those qualities can make it easy for you to test your dog for readiness to begin practical tracking.

Leave your dog in a comfortable place while you and your tracklayer check out one of the work areas you haven't used for a couple of days. You'll need a block big enough to lay a track approximately 65 feet long into with a space about 50 feet wide on both sides of it. Keep your chosen area free of your helper's scent until he lays the track. The two of you should review the diagram on the facing page.

It is important that you both understand all the factors that are illustrated in order to test your dog and come to appreciate the principle that can enable him to scout for tracks in a logical way. The sketch will show how a flag should be placed, by someone other than the tracklayer, so that orientation will be easy for the two of you. You will see how the tracklayer starts the test track into the wind on a course that takes him a yard to the left of the flag. One step, no more, after he passes the flag he will drop a sock of low visibility on the track and step on it; then continue on for a few more steps and drop a second sock to give the dog another opportunity for success, and to mark the end of the track. After another few steps, he should turn left and leave the area crosswind so that neither the track scent nor his body scent will be borne to you when you and your dog approach the track from the right.

There is a good reason why the tracklayer is told to end that track and clear the area such a short distance after he passes the flag. If the track would continue farther than necessary, there would be greater chance for a varying wind component to angle across the track and bring airborne scent to the dog as he gets close to the track which would make it unnecessary for him to do much scouting. At present, we want him to find the track that will lead him to the sock, and not merely use an errant wind that would lead him in a chance pattern before he has to make an effort. The test and diagram have shown you what the tracklayer should do. Now let's look at what you should do.

Let the track age for ten minutes, bring your dog directly crosswind from the right, and stop about 15 feet from the track on a heading that will take you a few feet downwind from the flag. Now put the harness on him and attach the line as a cue that it's time to go to work. Remove your leash, but leave the collar so you could correct him in the unlikely case such a need would occur.

Put him on a down-stay for the usual "focusing" time. The fact that you put him on a down-stay without a scent for him to memorize will not confuse him. It will be part of a cue for him to start using his nose. Go. Be quick to follow when he takes your command and starts in the direction you've aimed him.

In seconds he'll cross that 15 feet to the track. Even before he gets there, he could get into the wind pattern that bears the scent of the track. If the scent is faint, his previous experience will get his nose close to the track so the ground scent can lead him to something he should find. He'll easily find and follow the track's direction. Your right angle approach should have caused him to hit the scent a bit downward from the flag which means that he'll only have to work a short distance into the helpful wind before he gets to the sock. Move to him and take it when he picks it up, and be quick to praise him.

Again, the new part of the pattern was to scout and find the track: the easy task of following the track to the sock was simply more of what he has done many times. Have him track on to find the second sock to end the exercise.

If scent conditions are poor, your dog could possibly pass over the track without catching the scent. The location of the flag will tell you if this occurs; if he crosses the track without alerting, put tension on the line to stop his forward progress and cause him to work

A bit of evidence can help to verify a track.

around carefully for the ground scents that will surely be there to lead him to the sock.

If a shift in the wind brings the scent of the track or sock to him before he gets close to the course that was laid, and he angles to the track upwind of the flag and the first sock and gets the sock that was dropped at the track's end, you will still have to praise him for his success, although he didn't have to scout for it. As said before, the path of the scent could be wider than the actual track, so he might detect it a bit sooner than you anticipate.

In the very unlikely case that he goldbricked, appeared confused or otherwise ignored the track, it would be wrong to point to the track or the sock, or give a second verbal cue. Your dog's previous experience in "blind retrieving" makes it perfectly fair to expect him to go out on a single command and find a track that will lead him in a few seconds to something that he'll be praised for finding.

To rule out the luck factor that could make one test inconclusive, set up and work two more patterns that are identical to the above.

About this time you might ask why didn't we have the dog smell and handle an article that bears the tracklayer's scent, just as we did in the earlier stages of training. Although introducing the tracklayer's scent to the dog with an article he has handled would be another cue to track, and is sometimes used to give Bloodhounds and other dogs a clue as to the scent they should seek and follow, there is a good reason for omitting it as part of the preliminary when a dog is asked to scout for a track. In most emergency situations an article would not be available, thus that part of the cue-pattern would be missing, which might confuse a dog that had come to depend heavily on it. Secondly, information as to who handled an article last is often too vague to trust, and one might give a dog the scent of someone other than the person being sought.

Consistently use the cue of the harness, the down-stay and your regular verbal command to focus your dog and start him scouting. You'll always have them with you.

Don't start the next level of training if you experienced difficulty with the above test. Go back and work to achieve the things you need. Be honest in admitting your weak points so you'll be able to correct them.

You probably found the test to be easy, and are looking forward to developing yourself and your dog into a team that can successfully scout for tracks.

For your assurance that it should be easy and reasonable for a dog with good basic training, to go out on a single command and find a track that will lead him to articles that bear the tracklayer's scent, I would like to share some documentable facts with you.

One of the conditions that I have imposed on clubs that have sponsored the clinics and seminars that I have conducted all over the United States and some foreign countries is that they have available some dogs that were positively motivated retrievers so I could demonstrate my method of starting some of the Utility exercises. After an introduction to a strange object, the dog will be asked to retrieve it from where it was hidden from his sight in a hole or under grass cover. No second command or cue will be given, but a correction will be used in a rare case where the dog fails to search until successful.

Did I risk credence or embarrassment when I told large groups that such demands for "blind retrieves" were reasonable? Not really. Only a few times in these many demonstrations did these handlers of positively motivated retrievers encounter any problem in sending a dog for unseen objects. And you won't have a problem in sending your dog to find a track that will lead him to objects that bear the scent of the person who laid that track. So be glad your success is well founded and that you and your dog are prepared to develop real skill in scouting for tracks.

Being lost for a few hours can be a terrifying experience.

A big sister never looked better.

6

Scouting for Tracks

NO MATTER HOW EASILY your dog passed the foregoing test, it will be a mistake that will haunt you if you try to bridge over any of the following training blocks as unnecessary. It's true that your dog showed his understanding and responsibility when he moved out, cross wind, on your command and was rewarded with a find when his course took him to the track, and the wind told him its direction, and the track led him to the sock. But there is a difference between going out a short distance to achieve a quick success and moving out for hours and miles, all the time alert and aware of his responsibility. You are justified in asking how a dog, possibly not blessed with boundless enthusiasm, will hold that awareness for a long period, and when he finds a track, work to determine its direction and follow it to the best of his ability.

Let's see how even a deadhead can be changed to a dog with such great perseverance. There are two analogies that will help you understand why such a change can take place.

First, it's common knowledge that a person who starts a program of jogging or walking, even reluctantly, will develop a fervent need for such exercise, sometimes to the point where it could be called a healthy addiction. Regardless of how difficult and uninviting such a program is at the start, it seems to develop a learned need for the satisfaction it can provide.

Another example of how the appetite for expression can be developed by an activity that might initially be uninviting is found in the area of dog training. I have commented on the value of positive retrieving in several places in this book. Now I want to go a bit further so you will understand why your dog will persevere when he must work a long time to find a track.

First of all, bear in mind that the fallacy that the "natural and play-trained retrievers" work more happily than those that have been trained to work, regardless of their inclination at a given time, has long been debunked — due in part to performance in the obedience ring, and to those of us who offered the challenge of "comparison."

Although I had long been aware of the above truth, it was quite by chance that I noticed the degree to which individual dogs can be brought to the point of enjoying what they originally regarded as acceptable but uninviting. A number of us were watching the dogs in a Utility Class work on the "go-out" component of the Directed Jump exercise. Suddenly it occurred to all of us that of ten consecutive dogs that had run out the full distance to the ring's end, in the belief that unseen dowels might have been placed for them to retrieve, several of them had not been fast retrievers during their C.D.X. work. But now, instead of trotting to where there might have been dowels, they ran. Carefully planned increments wherein they had been compelled, regardless of their resistance, to go out gradually increased distances to hunt and retrieve hidden dowels, had instilled in them a need that they satisfied by doing a difficult job.

An equal need for satisfaction can be produced by following a structured approach to scouting for tracks.

You must gradually increase the distance he must scout from where you start him to where he is rewarded with the success of finding the track. The following schedule of progressions is reasonable.

Because this is primarily an exercise in going out into the unknown and finding a track, and determining which way it runs, it is important that, in the early stages, the dog finds the sock soon after he turns onto the track.

Therefore, there is no reason to lay long tracks for the early scouting exercises. It's better to work on the long tracks separately, where the dog is started on an indicated scent, and you will not owe him quick success as you do when he finds and starts a track. The

Children are sometimes lost for a few scary hours in big cornfields. The corn muffles their cries for help.

A pair of light binoculars can save lots of time when you're planning your scouting patterns.

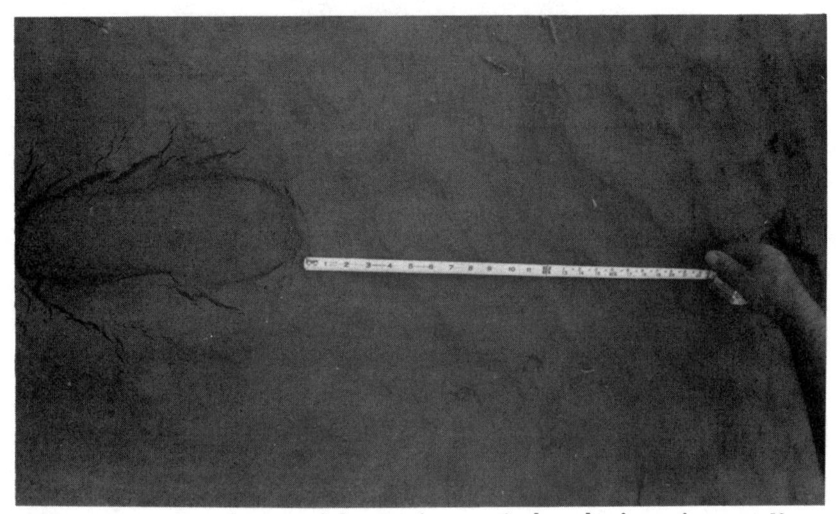

A tape measure can be a useful part of a practical tracker's equipment. Keep one in your pack.

concentration of success he'll experience will convince him that, when you send him, he can always find a track, and he should move out in front of you with confidence. He'll become addicted to it.

For five days scout only for tracks that run upwind so that when your dog cuts into them the scent will be blown toward him, not away from him. Continue with the same basic pattern you used to start and test your dog, with one exception. Each day increase the distance from where you send the dog to where the track lies by about 20 feet. If you should have a superdog and you're sure that such modest progressions are an affront to his great ability, control your enthusiasm and stay with the method. You'll be glad you did.

Work three such tracks each day. This program will be less time-consuming if your helper lays three tracks in areas close to each other, but avoiding any conflicts. The drawing on Page 80 will remind you to be very conscious of the wind factors. It will take only a few minutes to lay each track, and, because they'll all be aging at practically the same time, they'll all be ready to start within an hour.

After a couple of days of working on the righthanded approaches to the track, start giving him experience in bisecting similar upwind tracks when he approaches from the left side. By the end of the week he will have made many approaches, from both right and left, to where the wind brought the scent to him about the time he reached the track, which led him to quick success in getting the sock. With the short daily increases in distance, he now scouts 100 feet from where you start him to where the track lies.

LEVEL 1:
Finding and Turning Onto Downwind Tracks.

There are two good reasons why you should proceed step by step on the downwind setups, using the same increments of distance as you did when favorable winds helped the dog to note the track direction and led him to the sock. First, the downwind will be a hindrance, not a help, and most dogs can use practice in having to work close to the actual track where the ground scent originates. Second, you will be pleased to see how this close work will increase your dog's sustained responsibility against those inevitable times when he will have to work for long periods before he is rewarded by finding a track. So control any eagerness to skip progressions. Build a solid foundation.

As when you set the pattern for upwind tracks, a short track will be sufficient. Remember, the purpose of the scouting exercise is to find tracks and start them so your dog will be rewarded with prompt success and praise as he solves the problem. A flag should be set at each end of the track and another at approximately mid-course to provide the tracklayer and you with an aiming point. The tracklayer will need two socks or other articles. He will start the track at the upwind flag and lay a downwind track that passes close to the mid-course flag, and ends at the downwind flag. About ten feet downwind from the mid-course flag, no farther, he will drop a sock on the track and mash it close to the ground so it will not be seen before it is smelled. He will continue on to the final flag and drop the second sock, then clear out of the area.

Let the track age at least a half-hour so the body scent will dissipate and so your dog's scent source will be the track.

Bring him toward the track from the right, and stop when you're 15 feet from the course. Equip him with the harness and line, and start him as you have been doing. Aim him carefully at the mid-course flag, and start him.

If he intersects the track close to the flag, he'll be no more than 10 feet upwind from the sock. Obviously, any scent that the wind bears to him will be coming from the opposite direction to the track runs, and he is likely to test the track by backtracking a few feet. When the scent in the direction he moves gets weaker instead of stronger, he'll know he's heading wrong and turn back downwind, putting his nose close to the ground to catch the track scent at its source. After he's determined the direction, the scent beam will quickly lead him to the sock and a load of praise.

Now that he has found the direction it runs, let him work the track out to the final sock.

As on the upwind tracks give your dog practice on approaching the tracks from both the right and left sides.

LEVEL 2:
Crosswind Toward The Dog.

By now you've worked your dog crosswind, from right and left, to tracks that were laid into the wind; and to tracks laid downwind so the problems of determining and following the track's direction would be more difficult. In each of the above directions, the spectrum of scent would arise from the ground straight above the track. Now let's see what winds blowing straight across a track can do.

Refer to the drawing on Page 80 to help you draw out the effect of a crosswind that's blowing from a track toward your dog. You will see that it might bring him snatches of scent to lead him to where the track lies, but it certainly won't help him determine which way the track runs. When he does work out the direction of the track, he'll have to adjust to the fact that any airborne scent values will be on the leeward side of the track, and keep his nose down close to the ground where the scent originates if he is to follow the track efficiently.

The distance and the right angle of your approach to these tracks should be about the same as on the first two wind directions. Because the wind is carrying the scent toward your dog as he approaches the track, he will probably pick it up sooner than on the first problems, but you can expect he will need more time to work out the track's direction.

LEVEL 3:
Crosswind From Your Dog.

The least helpful wind of all is the wind that blows straight away from the dog as he scouts toward the track. Such a wind will not bring any airborne scent to tell him where the track lies, nor will it help him determine the direction it runs. In fact, with all the scent being blown away from him, he will probably be past the point where the scent originates before it is possible for him to smell it, unless he scouts with his nose close to the ground.

Except for the wind direction, work him as you did on the first three wind components, giving him an equal amount of experience, or more if you feel he needs it. The experience you'll get from working on these staged and marked tracks will help you understand your dog's moves and mannerisms when he's following an unmarked track, and the only information you get is what he gives you.

EVALUATE: You've spent 12 to 15 days of training on the four patterns that were used to relate wind components to tracks your dog found by scouting. True enough, those patterns always employed sharp angles, and when you are called upon to follow an unplanned track, you will have to contend with winds that relate to the track in an infinite number of angles. However, a dog that can work the sharp angles of relationship should have no difficulty in handling the more moderate angles. So if you give yourself and your dog lots of practice on sharp patterns of wind relationship, as shown on Page 80 you will both be well prepared for most winds that relate to the tracks you will follow.

You are the best judge of your dog's competence, and if you believe that the two of you are effective in finding and following tracks, and your dog no longer needs the immediate success that he has been getting when he finds a track, you can begin to increase the distance from where you send him to where he makes the find, and to put turns and changes of surface into the tracks, as you did on those tracks where he was started right on the scent.

But introduce these difficulties carefully and reasonably, so your dog will not have to work too long to gain success after he finds a track.

When your dog demonstrates an ability to reliably find and follow tracks, the general location of which are known to you, it will be time to start him scouting for tracks not marked with flags, and the exact location and direction of which are not known to you.

You will not observe as your helper lays a track similar to those you have been working.

Tell him to avoid any areas where he's laid a track within the previous two days. You won't watch, so there's no reason for you to be in the area before the track has aged a half-hour. He should drop a sock about every 50 feet on the track and a few steps after every turn he makes, and a sock to mark the track's end, so no matter where your dog finds and follows the track, he will be rewarded with at least one bit of success. Otherwise, if there were only one or two socks and your dog turned onto the track above where they were dropped, he would not find them, and neither he nor you will receive the confirmation of the track that will be helpful at this stage of training.

The tracklayer will set no flags nor will he tell you the precise location nor the direction of the track he has laid. Obviously you will be told the general area where the track lies, as would be the case when you would be told where a lost child was last seen or where a fugitive fled from a crime. The world is a big place and you will never be asked to start a search without knowing the general area where a track originated.

There are some things you should do when you arrive at the starting place. Very carefully note the direction, velocity and regularity of the wind. Scan the area where you will begin for physical features that would eliminate places where tracks could not be laid, such as inpenetrable cactus, deep water and other physical barriers that would exclude tracks in training and in emergency searches.

In studying any search problem the first consideration is how to play percentages so your start is addressed to the highest probabilities.

If practical, start at one side of area at the extreme downwind end if there is a discernible air movement. Sight on a tree, rock, or other mark on the far side of the area and note any other objects available for reference as you begin to work in a straight line toward the marker you've selected. The "ladder" illustration on Page 96 will show you how such a course relates to the area. When you reach the marker, move up a short distance, depending on the wind and the proficiency your dog has shown in detecting tracks under similar conditions. Focus on another reference point back on the starting side of area and start your next cast. The careful sighting is very important. Few people can walk in a straight line across a big field unless they focus on a marker.

You must be aware of your dog's casual whim to go off course and work the wind and the more positive way he'll act when he alerts on the scent of a track. If you've sacked him off distractions, you can be quite sure it's a human's track.

No-Wind Conditions

There will be times when there is no discernible air movement, and there will be no help from even a slow drift of scent. Remember this: The aura of scent does not rise in a narrow column, but where there is no horizontal air movement, rolls out in all directions.

At such times, work back and forth across the general area, where a track is known to lie, in casts spaced so that your dog is certain to come close to any scent that radiates from the track. Now your own concentration and skill will be more important than when

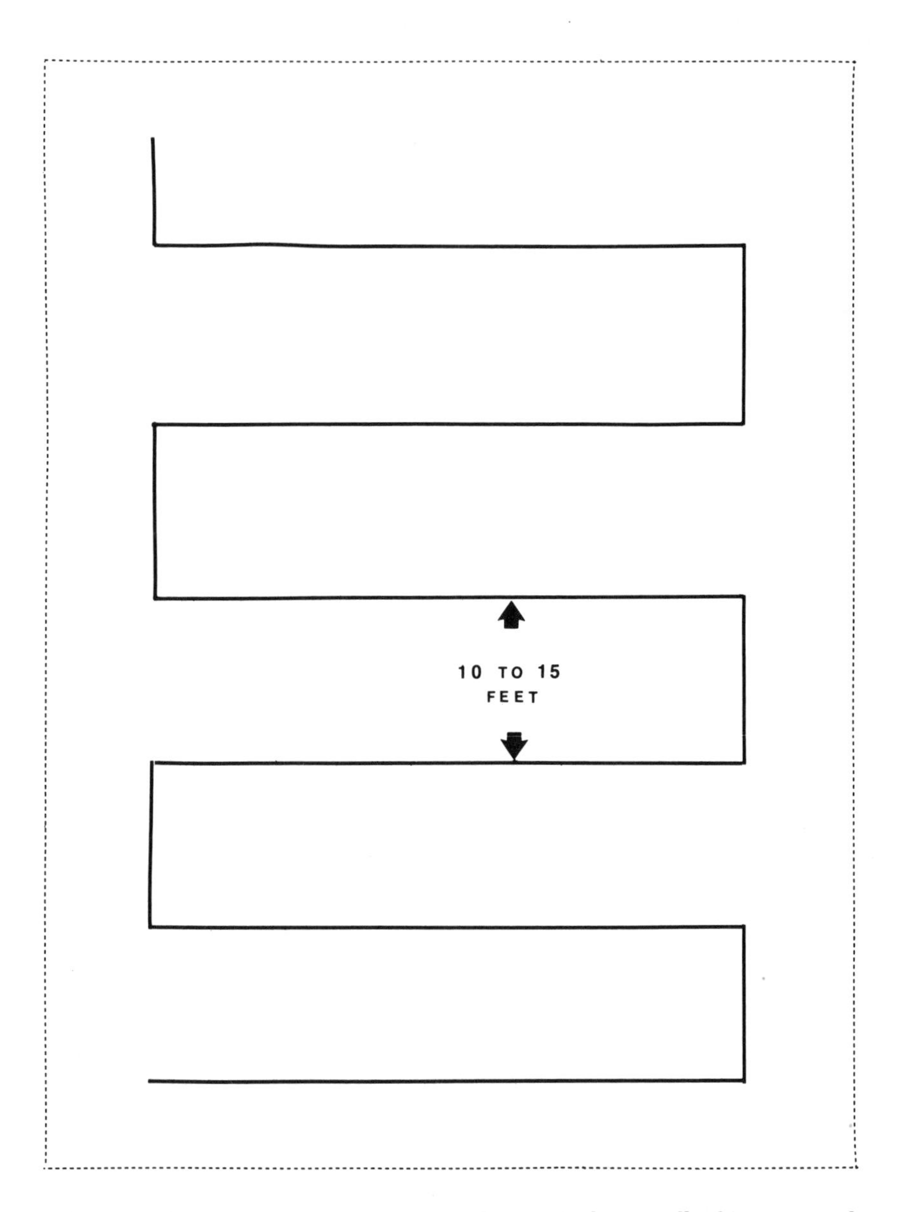

When scouting for the track of a person known to have walked in a general area, use a ladder-pattern instead of a quartering pattern such as is used to work a scout dog on body scent. Obviously, the steps will not be as precise as those shown in the drawing, but the space between the casts should be the same, approximately 10 to 15 feet.

favorable winds move the scent in such a way that your dog can detect it over a long distance.

Whether it's windy or still, when you reach the far side of the area, move up a logical distance and again select markers to guide you on a return course across the area. Percentages favor this "ladder" pattern over a shallow "quartering" pattern that might space the start of each successive cast unnecessarily close to the position of the previous cast. The purpose is to work the ground as thoroughly as needed but as rapidly as possible. Concentrate on working a good pattern so your dog is certain to come close to any track scent. Even though you won't always be able to understand the conditions that give your dog problems, you will be able to help him by progressing across an area with small bites that are certain to bring him close to a scent source. Take pains to read your dog correctly, and have confidence in his ability. Your experience on some of the earlier marked tracks should have shown you the great distance at which a dog can catch a scent when conditions are favorable. Believe him if he makes a definite alert even on one of the first casts across the area. If his cast is nonproductive, ease him back to your former course. Don't leave big gaps in your casting pattern.

If the pattern of your first blind-scouting area is similar to the sample diagram on the facing page, the casts should take your dog within scenting distance of any track that is laid within the perimeter. When he hits the track, the dog's work and your handling should be just as it was on all those problems where the track location had been staked.

Work at least three of these scouting exercises during the week, using similar area dimensions. Your difficulty and the time needed will vary from track to track as the scent conditions change. You'll need the experience the varied conditions will bring. Work for more than a week in the relatively small areas if you need extra practice in reading your dog. Get the confidence that comes from sufficient work before you attempt the next level.

The significant change from the previous level will be to increase the dimensions of the general areas where your blind-tracks will be laid. Working larger areas will mean your dog will need more of that quality that distinguishes the better practical tracking dogs. Perseverance. As you study the diagram on the facing page, you will see that the spot where a dog would locate a track in the big area is quite unpredictable. However, once he finds the track in the big areas, he can determine the direction it runs just as easily as he did in the small areas. And note that anywhere he finds the track it will lead him to the sock, or any other article you use, within a reasonable distance. Regardless of the point where your dog finds and follows one of these blind tracks, he should continue on the track to the last article, but no farther at this level.

At times he will hit near the start of the track and have the responsibility of finding all of the objects dropped for him. At other times scouting will take him to the track close to its end, and he will follow it only a short way and find only the final object. Bear in mind that your pattern of scouting an area is not the only thing that will affect the time it will take for your dog to hit and straighten out a track. Unfavorable conditions can cause him to miss a track at a time when he's very close to it. At other times a favorable breeze will bring the track scent to him from an unpredictable angle and over a surprising distance. Yes, luck plays a part, but the unpredictable factors are another reason why you should continue to learn how to read your dog and trust him.

The environment available for work areas will differ with each person who trains a dog, so don't expect this book to supply detailed track plans as you and your dog learn from working longer and more difficult problems. You and your tracklayer must do that job.

Obviously the exact route of the track will be decided without your knowledge, but there is some planning that the two of you will do together. The two of you should always visit any area you will use for practice scouting and decide on the boundaries of that section where the tracks will lie. From then on it will be the job of your helper to lay the track, and you and your dog will have the job of finding it.

Work your dog in so many different scouting areas and under such a variety of conditions that it seems the two of you are a team that can find any track your tracklayer lays, regardless of its pattern and relation to the wind.

It's now time to lengthen the aging period of the tracks. This is where your earlier experience and good judgment must govern your decisions. If you have tested his ability by having him work simple tracks, each a bit longer than the previous ones, you are the person best able to judge his ability on the colder tracks. But proceed cautiously, adding only a few minutes to the aging time of each successive track. Be careful to do your testing under varied conditions before you write your dog off as a "no-nose." There could have been some difficulties that you're not aware of. As mentioned earlier, you will always know the general area where a track lies. You will always be told the general area where a lost child or a fugitive was last seen. No rational person would ask you to guess at the part of the world where you should scout for a track.

As you and your helper select areas where he will lay tracks, remember to vary the surface and cover. Take advantage of changes in the weather so your dog gets practice under those conditions. Lost kids and fugitives don't lay tracks only when conditions are favorable.

In addition to the short tracks your dog has found by scouting, you gave him experience on those long and difficult tracks on which you started him right on the scent in the conventional way. It is now time to combine the skill of finding tracks with his ability to follow those tracks even when they're difficult.

Until now your tracklayer has dropped a "marker" each time he left the scouting area, and when your dog found it you praised him to end his job, then put him on leash and took him from the area. Realistically, there will always be an area where you will start your dog so such fundamental practice is essential to practical tracking. But now it's time to consider another reality. Tracks that are started in a general area will often quickly lead into a radically different kind of terrain, as the track of a lost child that leads from an open field into dense brush. Most of the practice that goes into tracking for titles fails to condition a dog to meet radical changes. This failure is easily understood because tracking tests must be staged with similar conditions for each competing dog, and in full view of the judges.

To give your dog needed practice in meeting the demands that are part of practical tracking, select some scouting areas that are immediately adjacent to radical changes. Fields with light vegetation that border on brushy areas is one example. Tracks that are found in the woods and run across roads to open fields is another realistic situation.

When working in these contrasting environments, your tracklayer will no longer drop the marker as he is about to leave the scouting area, but will drop it a short distance after he enters the contrasting area. Discuss the conditions with him so the dog won't be asked to work too long on the first few departure tracks before he finds the sock and you can praise him for a job well done. The distance he'll have to follow a track before it leaves the scouting area is unpredictable, so keep the exit track short. Fifty feet from the scouting area out into the new ground and on to the last sock should be about right at the start.

Work in the above pattern for as many tracks as it takes for you and your dog to show competence and confidence, then begin to lengthen the exit tracks.

Plan carefully as you extend the tracks and make conditions a bit more difficult with turns and changes of terrain. Increase the distance between the socks dropped in the scouting area and have the marker dropped farther out on the exit track to end your dog's work.

Don't mug your dog with words by constantly chattering what you feel is encouragement just because the tracks are getting more difficult. Such yakking is generally more distracting than encouraging. If difficulties on the long tracks seem to discourage him it's probably because you got over-eager and left some goofing gaps in your early training. Chatter will not hold his mind on an honest effort, but there is something you must remember. Crossing a stream, sliding down banks and other physical interruptions can temporarily surplant a dog's feeling of responsibility, and in such situations the repetition of a command or other encouragement to diminish the interruption and return him to responsibility might be needed.

As you increase the length of the exit track from the scouting area to the last sock that ends the track, it's inevitable that the time demanded will cause you to reduce the number of tracks you'll work. Fortunately, tracking can be done, and should be done, at varied hours of the day and in all kinds of weather, so you should be able to find a time slot for at least two tracks each week. Routine exercises done at scheduled times are helpful at some levels of dog training, but they're unrealistic for a tracking dog that might be called upon at any hour in any weather.

Your dedication, your dog's ability, and other factors will determine how rapidly you will increase the track lengths. Actually, you handled tracks that were 2000 yards long while you were working on the fundamentals presented in this book.

The big difference between those tracks and the blind tracks that challenge your dog at this level is the absence of a known starting place and marking flags. The socks on the track indicate when your dog is right, but such confirmation comes after he tracks to them, not as prior indicators that he is heading right. Generally you will not see the socks until he leads you to them. And he will lead you to a deep appreciation of his wonderful nose.

By the time your dog is performing reliably at the level of practical tracking, you will probably feel two distinct emotions in quick order. First, you'll be elated as you realize that you and your dog could find and follow the blind track of a lost child. Second, you will be concerned with how you might know for certain that the track your dog finds and follows is that of the person you seek.

Although there are few absolutes that relate to emergency situations, you will be surprised to know of all the percentages that you can use to verify that your dog has found and is following the "right" track. The first two chapters of this book were devoted to getting your dog to use his nose. The next chapter will help you to use your mind and powers of observation in ways that will help, not hamper, your dog.

There are three dim tracks in this picture. Note all of the differences.

7

Verifying a Track

ONE OF THE DIFFERENCES between tracking in a formal test and practical tracking is that in the latter activity you will need to verify that the track your dog finds is the "right" one. There will be no marker to indicate the start of a track, and no flags to tell you that, at least for a short distance, your dog has the scent. But cheer up. There is much information on the ground to verify whether a track is that of the man, woman or child you seek.

Perhaps the most harmful misconception of how to verify a track is the fallacy that one should concentrate on seeking objects that are dropped by trackers who followed the advice of "guessers" who told them to regard dropped articles as the best source of information on the one whose track they are following. It was called to my attention that one book goes so far as to advise locating the track itself by first finding a dropped object.

Far more plentiful and important than objects dropped on a track is something else a tracklayer is sure to leave. This is what the visual trackers call "sign." Not signs. Jack Kearney, a Supervisory Border Patrol agent of the El Cajon, California Border Patrol Station is involved with other agents in an operation that is probably the most impressive example of sight-tracking in history. To those persons not aware of the tens of thousands of illegal aliens that pour over California's Southern border, the number of man-tracks these agents successfully follow is beyond comprehension. This is done with visual tracking, without the aid of dogs. I am very

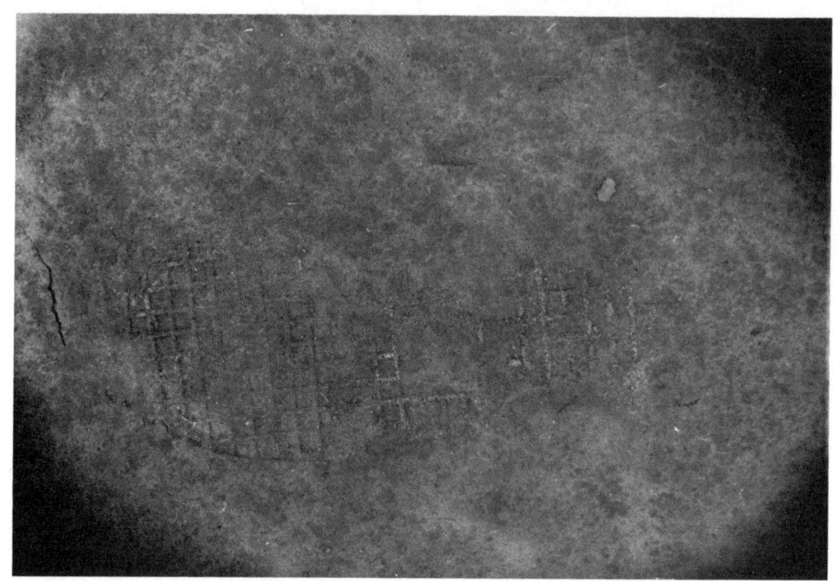

The size and treadmarks of a shoe can tell you much about the anatomy of the person you are tracking.

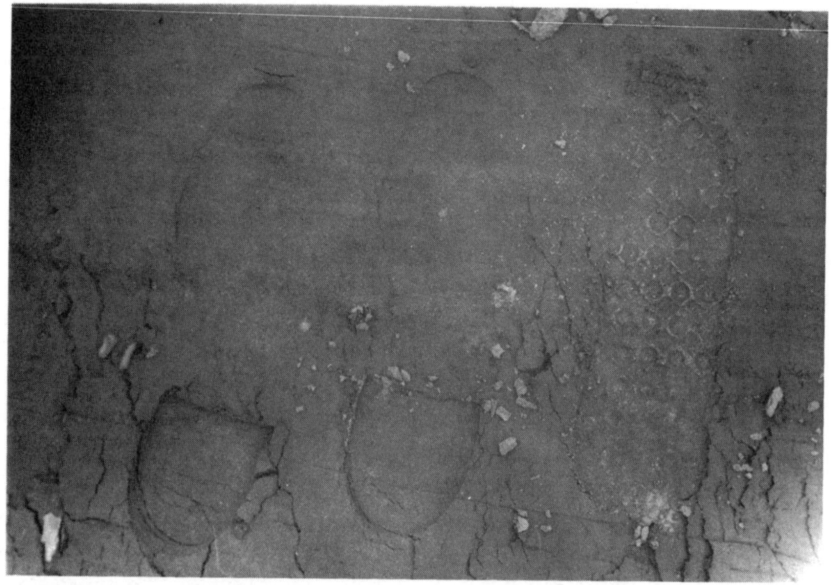

Jogging shoe, work shoe, and dress shoe. Practice will help you find the distinctive marks.

familiar with one instance where a Border Patrol Station considered the use of dogs, but ran into bleeding-heart pressure against the "inhumane" proposal to track people with dogs, although there are instances when the lives of aliens were saved when they were found by the Border Patrol.

The high ratio of success achieved by the Border Patrol Agents in their own field, and when they assist other groups in search and rescue, is proof of the sign that any tracklayer leaves. If these agents can develop the skill to follow a track without the help of a dog's nose, you can learn to observe the many indicators that your dog will lead you to, and which will tell you much about the person who made the track. From familiarity with the area in which the El Cajon agents do their job, I would say your environment will be easier to work.

The Border Patrol agents regard objects found on a track as relatively unimportant to their success in following that track. They rely on the sign that is always present on a track. This is easily understood. Jack Kearney estimates that only one object will be dropped for every three miles of track. In view of the above fact from a qualified source, you might ask how anyone could ask a handler and dog to find a track by wandering around looking for a small dropped object, instead of scouting for a long, continuous ribbon of scent.

Any track your dog follows can tell you something about the person who made it. Even part of a footprint can indicate the size of its maker. The depth of the heel mark will show whether it was made by a light or heavy person. If there has not been any recent rainfall, and your own footprint impresses the soil more deeply than the print of the one you are following, he is probably lighter than you. If your print is more shallow than his, he's heavier. If you know how heavy you are, you can make a good guess at the weight of the tracklayer. There are many other ways in which attentiveness and logic can help you verify a track. The pictures in this chapter should help you learn to verify a track.

Sometimes it is possible to rule out a track your dog is on by reconciling time and distance. For example, if your dog finds a track at a point more than three miles from where a five-year-old child you seek was seen less than two hours before your dog's "find," logic and experience will tell you it was probably not the right track. Unless you find other visual sign that verifies the track beyond any doubt, it would be well to take the dog properly from the track and resume scouting.

Often, the environmental features of an area where your dog is tracking can tell you some things. If a track runs in a straight line under low limbs or an arbor of brush only a few feet above the ground, you might assume it was made by a short person.

Some kinds of steep terrain would feature handholds that could only be used by a tall, strong person. Unless you've positively verified a track, don't follow it over ground that the subject of your search would have extreme difficulty in negotiating.

When a track leads you to a height or vantage point, look to see if there is an obvious place to where a tracklayer would be heading, or if he makes an obvious turn away to avoid it. Such sign will indicate whether he wants to be discovered or would rather not be seen, and can spell out the difference between a lost person or a fugitive.

The best and most enjoyable way of learning to see and interpret the abundance of visible information on a track is to study and practice without your dog to guide you. Have someone lay short tracks of fifty to seventy yards under varying conditions of soil and vegetation. They should not be so difficult that you can hardly follow them at first, nor should they be so easy that there is no learning experience.

You'll soon gain two things: rapidly growing confidence in your ability to use your eyes and mind, and a deep appreciation of how much more easily your dog's nose could have unraveled those tracks for you.

You can make sure the learning and practice sessions are a lot of fun if you work with someone who shares your enthusiasm. Select a person who seeks more mental and physical challenges than he can get from twisting a TV dial. Plan some tracks that will provide the needed learning experience and which are equal in such a way as to provide fair competition between the two of you in following them at each level of difficulty. When you become fascinated, and you will, with all the stories an environment tells an observant person, you can get a first hand account of how Border Patrol agents learn to read signs. Jack Kearney wrote an excellent book, available from the publisher, Pathways Press, 525 Jeffres Street, El Cajon,

When verifying a track that runs up a steep path, you will have only the depth and form of the marks to indicate the size and weight of the tracklayer.

On light down-grades, heel marks will often be quite plain.

How many tracks are in this picture?

California 92023. Jack Kearney's book will be of particular interest to all peace officers.

Regardless of how well you learn to use your eyes, don't ever forget that the purpose of your skill is to verify whether the track your dog is following is that of the person you seek. Never use that skill to second-guess your dog's ability to track. His nose can detect what no eyes can see.

While her family was moving into their new home on Whidbey Island, Washington, a little girl crossed this road and was lost for hours while the people of the area searched frantically. A good dog could have found her in a short time.

8

Problems

OFTEN a professional trainer will be asked how to solve an obedience problem relating to poor or erratic performance in a specific situation. An answer might be given only to be met with the protest, "But you don't understand my problem,"—such as comes from a simplistic soul who seeks an instant solution, and cannot comprehend how fundamentals relate to a dog that won't do "what he knows very well he should do."

This same rejection of basic truths is often the case with inexperienced trainers who have problems with tracking-dogs. True, some dogs have less ability or are slower to comprehend than others, but let's run a check list of the basics before you conclude you have a problem that is unrelated to fundamentals.

There is a whole group of tracking problems which results from weak motivation, tentative, infirm handling, or by failing to work and practice at a level until the dog is performing reliably and happily before advancing to the next step. Remember, when you have to back up a step it's easier to do so when there's a good solid step to stand on. Here are some of the most common problems in that group:

1. Slow start and lack of prompt concentration.
2. Dog is affected by environmental distractions that occur.
3. Lacks determination to work out turns and more difficult parts of the track.

4. Wants to quit when the ground or cover is a bit uncomfortable.
5. Lacks sustained drive on long tracks.

In nearly every instance the solution to the above problems is not to bridge across them with vittles and vascillation, but to face up to the fact that you didn't honestly instill responsibility when your dog was working close to you and he couldn't "con" you. The answer is not only to "go back" and retrace the fundamentals, but to challenge him at each level until he's past contention and you'd bet the farm that he'll try his best.

Poor Handling

Poor handling nearly always results from insufficient work on a variety of thoughtfully staged tracks so a dog will acquire the needed recognition of varied conditions, and so you will become adept at reading him, and be fair in your evaluation of what he is experiencing and can handle effectively. This is why the author emphasizes the need to use carefully planned tracks so you can set the challenges and watch the dog handle the conditions you've staged.

Turns

If your dog seems to find it difficult to believe that a track can turn, even when the wind draws him a picture, there is a simple aid that can help even the most rigid "tunnel-nose." It's the process of using tracks laid in such shallow bends that they lead the dog only slightly to the right or left, similar to those shown in the drawing on the facing page. If practiced enough, such tracks will beckon his nose to such small changes in direction that it's inconceivable that a responsible dog would have difficulty in following the scent. Such practice will instill a subconscious awareness of the fact that tracks do turn. After he shows that awareness, increase the amount of the bend. Very gradually. If he had difficulty with the early work on tracks that turned into the wind that brought the scent to him, he's probably oriented to ground scent and will not be helped nor hindered by wind direction, so you need not lay the tracks to favor the wind. Sufficient practice on the above patterns will help him solve the turns: insufficient practice will not.

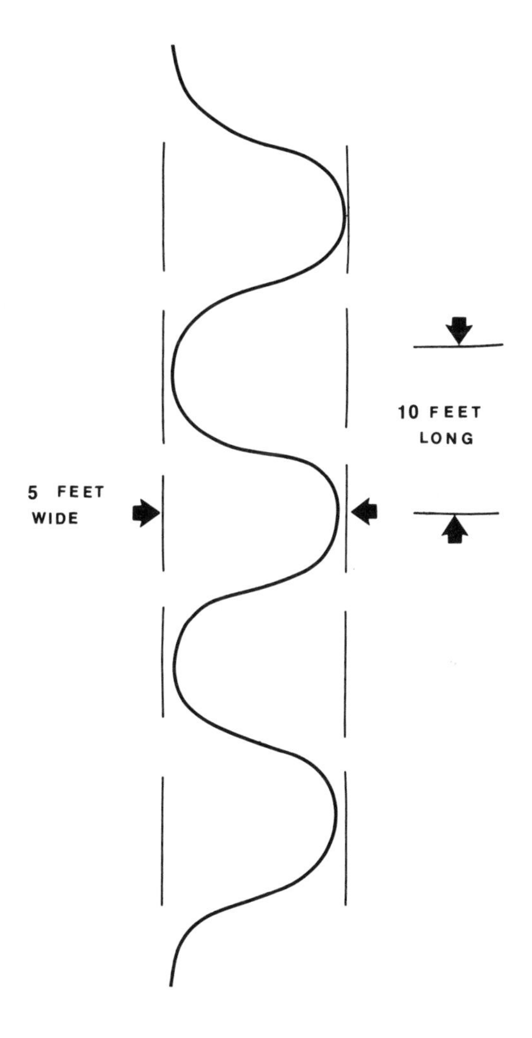

If your dog is a "tunnel-nose," gentle bends in short tracks will beckon him to the right and left, so he'll learn that tracks sometimes turn.

The author's boyhood experience in tracking was with hunting dogs. The author (right) and his buddy, Art Stumbaugh, spent all their available time in the woods and fields.

Possible Poor Scenting Ability

If you suspect that your dog's nose might be inadequate, there is a way to check his ability easily and accurately. But first be sure he's motivated to do his best.

We know that the dog's olfactory ability is phenomenal. We also know that there is quite a variation in that ability even among dogs that are bred for the job.

Experienced hound men will tell you that in a pack of hounds there is often one dog that finds it easier than others to follow cold tracks. The author has had years of experience in training upland hunting dogs, and, when working on planted birds, has observed the exact distance that a dog has a scent in comparison with other dogs. There is sometimes a dog with an inferior nose. When observing and evaluating scout dogs for the military, careful records were kept on scenting-ability as an aid to certifying a dog for actual service.

You can determine whether your dog's nose is below par by this same process of comparing his performance with that of some other dogs when all are worked under the same conditions. Don't base your evaluation on one or two tests. Make several comparisons. You can get another good reading on his ability by letting another good handler work him on your own track.

Lay several tracks yourself that are as similar as you can make them. Be in a position to watch unobserved while someone works your dog. Watch the other dogs work on the other tracks you laid, and compare your dog's performance with theirs. Certainly your dog had more reason to be interested in your scent than the other dogs did, and if his performance was inferior to theirs, there is good reason to believe his ability is less.

Just what do you do if all these tests prove he does not have a good nose? Nothing at all, except to make sure he's in good physical condition. There is some evidence that the keenness of the sense of smell will vary some with the state of a dog's health.

If you're deeply interested in tracking, you can increase the probability of getting a good prospect by considering a pup from a breed and family that has shown exceptional ability in scent work. The pedigrees of some of the hunting breeds and of some of the German working dogs record such performance. You'll learn a lot and have fun if you should make such a search.

The end of the trail.

9

Unusual Conditions

ALMOST EVERYONE who has begun to work with a tracking-dog has heard positive, but unqualified, statements made on how certain conditions of surfaces and atmosphere can make it impossible for any dog to follow a track. Much of the time these statements are only quoted opinions. It is unfortunate that the wide acceptance of such statements discourages experimentation, even by those who have dogs with great potential. These same newcomers are often inordinately involved with seeking answers in interesting, but seldom applicable, scientific investigations of the consistency of scent and the physiology of a dog's nose, all this at the expense of the time needed for a realistic and unwavering approach to motivating a dog.

Following are a few references to dogs performing under unusual conditions, and more importantly some suggestions on how you might test your own dog in comparison with others.

The most illuminating example of a dog's ability to detect an object by scent is when he dives deeply below the surface of the water and retrieves something that has sunk to a place among objects almost identical in size and form. That good water dogs can do this with the utmost reliability is a fact long known to those who have dogs that are almost as much at home in water as they are on land. Until recently this fact was not acknowledged by "scientists" who theorized on how scent was transported to a dog's nose "through the air" and identified by the dog as the specific scent he was seeking.

Perhaps all persons interested in scent are aware of the many cases where a Bloodhound has detected the scent of a body that was hidden far below the surface of the water, and which reveals its presence to the dog's nose by constantly emanating scent up to the open air. There is nothing in such a performance that contradicts the scientific concepts of a dog's ability and limitations. In fact, science has done much to determine the extent to which a dog can detect a percentage of scent in a proportionately huge volume of water. But the example of a dog going deep to identify by scent a small stone is functionally different. In the latter situation both the source of the scent and the dog's nose are under water. This means the scent was not transported to the dog through the air. Before one rushes to a conclusion on how the dog is able to perform the above feat, there is something he should know. The dog can do the same thing in the moving water of a stream.

"But," you might be thinking, "my dog won't be tracking with his head under water."

Probably not; but most dogs that track do become involved with water in one situation or another. Let's take a look at a few wet environments.

Rain

Moderate rainfall on level ground, where there is not a washing or bleaching factor, does not have much effect on the quality of a reasonably fresh track, but a deluge and time can erase the scent on a surface just as it erodes the surface on which it lies. It's been observed that a track laid on arid ground can be rejuvenated by a subsequent shower or a heavy dew.

Puddle, Ponds and Streams

As is demonstrated when a dog retrieves a pebble under water, there is a way that a scent-source can be detected through a medium other than air. We know that a dog can follow a fresh track laid through shallow water even when there is no vegetation to trap body scent left above the surface by the tracklayer. We know that time enables water to dilute and disperse the scent of a track much faster than it would the scent of a generative source, such as decaying organisms or aromatic materials. Obviously, when a track leads into moving water, it's best to cast for the emergence point, relying on visual sign and logistics, as well as your dog's nose.

Cold Tracks

The amazing account of Captain V. G. Mullikin's Bloodhound, Nick Carter, who followed a track that was 105 hours old, is but one of the true stories that tell of a dog's marvelous nose. Earlier in this book mention is made of a Doberman Pinscher that, according to *Guiness Book of Records,* followed a track across the South African Veldt for over 100 miles. There are many other examples of the cold-trailing ability that individual dogs have. The question so often asked is, "Just how much difference is there in the cold-trailing ability from one dog to another?"

Trials have been run for Bloodhounds in the United States and other places, and are still run occasionally. The American Kennel Club and some Schutzhund groups regulate and support tracking tests. There are "tree and line races" for trial hounds. But none of these enjoyable activities provide a means to test and compare the cold-trailing abilities of their dogs. In most of their trials it would be difficult to provide tracks sufficiently and uniformly aged to test and compare dogs.

But there is one group of enthusiasts who successfully put the running and observing of their dogs' ability before such trivialities as jobs, families and businesses. These are the owners of hunting hounds, generally tree-dogs, who often run their dogs in packs, and are in a position to find out which are the best strike-dogs and which are the best cold-trailers.

Significantly, their repeated observations, knowledge of animal habits, combined with visual findings indicates the approximate age of the tracks their dogs follow. These hunters will tell you that there is a vast and consistent difference between a good cold-nose dog and many others who try just as hard.

Dan Mannix, in his award-winning novel, *The Fox And The Hound,* featured a cross between a hound and a Pitbull Terrier. I sense that he named his character after "Copper," a renowned cold-trailing dog belonging to B. Adkins, the professional hunter featured in some of Mr. Mannix's articles in *Sports Illustrated* and *The Saturday Evening Post.*

I bred the Bull Terrier bitch, "Tinker" that Adkins ran with his hounds as a fighter, and became acquainted with him, and am grateful for bits of knowledge that he shared with me.

Two of the facts he shared should be important to anyone interested in the mysterious variances in dogs and conditions that one encounters in practical tracking. First of all, Adkins, a puzzled look on his weathered face, told me, "I've seen tracks Copper couldn't follow when they were so fresh I could almost smell 'em myself, and it seemed everything was just right for trackin'." Other mysteries that B. Adkins recalled had to do with his experiences on the deserts of Sonora, Mexico. "Somebody down there bred some stringy Bloodhounds that could follow tracks that other dogs couldn't even smell."

Remember, these mysteries of scent were related by a man who kept from fifty to sixty hounds, so he'd always have "a pack of half-dozen good ones," and who owned a cold-tracker internationally known for his ability.

What value does the corollary of the above difference in dogs and conditions have for the person who wishes to test his dog under varied conditions and ages of tracks? It's a reminder that you should test repeatedly under any condition where your dog experiences difficulty, and compare his performance with that of other dogs tested in the same way. A subsequent success can show you that previous failures were not necessarily due to lack of ability, but rather to mysterious conditions that are not understood. By such means you can determine your dog's abilities and limitations in a rational manner, and not judge him on his performance on a single day.

Moist Versus Dry

There are many beliefs relating to tracking so unfounded that they can qualify as phenomenons. Many of the wild guesses can be explained by the complete disregard that trainers involved only in man-tracking seem to have for the vast experience of hunters, who run hounds on a variety of game and under all conceivable conditions. Books on tracking rarely mention the sources of their knowledge about "where and when" dogs supposedly cannot track. What hunters have learned can have value to all of us whether our pleasure comes from tracking game or men.

One of the beliefs accepted by many, but not all, hound men, is that moist ground is always more favorable to tracking than dry ground. Although I was involved with hunting hounds from boyhood, my early hunting was done on moist and well vegetated surfaces, and I shared the belief that it was always difficult for a dog to follow a track on extremely dry ground. It was many years later that I learned differently from my friend, Lloyd Beebe.

Anyone who has followed Lloyd on snowshoes will tell you he is quite an outdoorsman. Lloyd is an award-winning cinema photographer who has worked from the Antarctic to the Arctic, and in swamps, mountains and deserts.

It was when Walt Disney produced *The Legend of Lobo,* which featured a lot of wolves, that Lloyd took his pack of hounds from Washington's moist Olympic Peninsula to sun-baked Arizona, and started another big discussion on "moist versus dry." Because the production called for a pack of hounds it was natural for Lloyd to use his own dogs. And when the production date was delayed a bit, it was natural for Lloyd and his friend, Del Ray, to do a little hunting. Hunters who had run hounds in the desert country had prophesized nationally that "if Beebe ever brought his hounds from their familiar moist home area in Washington to arid Arizona, they'd find out what tough tracking was, and probably act like they had plugs in their noses."

Lloyd's hounds were not affected by the prophesies. The number of cougars they treed in a three week period was outstanding, and the statements on the positive effects of "damp and dry" were retracted in puzzled tones in a national trailhound magazine. (Don't pity the cougars. Lloyd is a renowned conservationist, and operates The Olympic Game Farm, and once they were treed, the cougars were left to their own devices.)

I put the "damp and dry" question to Lloyd one day when we were working on a Walt Disney production. He answered me with an analogy I would like to quote: "If you come into a room where everyone's talking," Lloyd said in his quiet way, "you can speak in a real loud voice and the others can hardly hear you. But if you come into a room where no one's talking, you can almost whisper and most others in the room can hear you. Maybe it's the same with tracks on cool, damp ground where there are lots of animals. The scent holds so well there that there could be a whole bunch of tracks for a hound to sort out. On a hot desert, where not as many animals have traveled, a hound can take the faintest snatches of scent as being part of the right track. It's probably the only track around."

Later, Lloyd shared another bit of provocative logic with me: "When a track is laid on a wet surface, it leaves some of its scent in the moisture; and when the moisture evaporates, some of the scent goes with it. Scent laid on dry ground is affected by time and air, but no part of the retaining surface is removed by evaporation."

If you want to make your own comparisons of the retention of scent by a wet and dry surface, you will find the following details helpful.

John G. Helleis, of LaVerne, California, used his Brittany, Ch. Sir Jacob of Rey River Ranch, U.D., P.C. in carefully staged tests to see how well scent was retained on aluminum scent-articles when one of them was scented while wet and the other when dry.

The two scented articles were placed among three identical articles that were unscented. Each day over the 11-day period the articles were placed on different surfaces so that the scent-combinations would vary, including grass, gravel, pavement, etc. He rubbed one of the articles that was dry and the other while it was moist, and placed the two of them among the three unscented articles. Observation was made as to which article retained the scent better by gradually lengthening the aging period.

During the first few days, when the scent had aged only a few hours, the dog could identify either article with equal ease. But as the period was extended to more than 12 hours, it was definitely easier for the dog to detect the article that had been scented when dry, indicating that some of the scent that had been applied over moisture had depreciated more rapidly than the scent that had been deposited on a dry surface.

As a matter of interest, the time of detecting and retrieving the correct articles averaged five seconds, even when the aging period was extended to 24 hours.

Simply put, when the moisture goes, some of the scent mixed with it goes along.

1
4

The Effects of Surface Texture

The surface upon which a track is laid is not as significant for its capacity to receive scent as it is for its capacity to *retain* scent. The pockets and depressions in earthen surfaces, whether vegetated or bare, are little traps and baffles that hold scent against the sweep of air currents. Smooth pavement or rock will receive the scent equally well but without those "traps" will not hold it as long. A practical tracker might be called upon to track on such surfaces, so give your dog experience on the smooth pavements, gradually lengthening the aging time until you find the extent of your dog's ability.

The Aromatic Surface

There has been much theorizing on how some aromatic surfaces can affect the performance of a dog who tracks across them. The aromas can be from organic materials such as eucalyptus leaves, creosote bushes, pine needles, and other pungent vegetable matter, or from chemicals in pavements and other treated areas. Dogs used for search and rescue and for police departments often must work under such conditions, so consideration of the matter is important. Those conditions vary from one part of the country to another. For example, Iowa doesn't have pine forests or creosote bushes, but it has large fields treated with fertilizers, organic and chemical.

One surface condition that exists almost universally is the paved parking lot that surrounds all shopping centers. It's safe to say that most stores burglarized are located in such situations, and a dog used to assist police in finding the direction of departure will have to work on pavement.

Practice and observe your dog on such surfaces as he might have to work. You might be pleasantly surprised at how well he does, and enjoy his accomplishments even if you don't plan to use him in practical tracking.

10

The Tracking Police Dog

THE PATH of a peace officer often leads him into situations that are unfair. At times it seems the efforts of the courts and some organizations not only make his work more difficult, but relegate his right to protect his own life to something inconsequential. Fortunately, good dogs are providing an increasing number of policemen with something of an equalizer.

Such a dog can make a policeman's life a bit easier during those times when he's dealing with a suspect who resists arrest; and the more intelligent city officials are starting to recognize that a dog can protect a city against suit at the same time he's aiding an officer. A dog with a threatening appearance can cause a suspect to reveal any weapon he might have as he faces an animal that might not be familiar with all "the rules." Once that weapon is produced, the policeman is forewarned and he can draw and use his own weapon with less chance of later investigations and heart-rending cries of "unjustified force." Hopefully, we are not yet at a point where a court would expect him to see which way a bullet goes before reacting.

Also, the public is as slow to blame a dog if a suspect's actions earn him a stabilizing bite as it is to blame a horse when a hoof accidentally mashes a rioter's foot when the horse is working on crowd control.

In both cases there is the "probability" that the four-footed ally acted on his own initiative. When questioned by a court, dogs and horses will seldom contradict such an opinion.

If a police dog has enough aggressiveness and enjoys combat, his eagerness will motivate him to be exceptional in the work of detection. Unique sensing abilities enable him to quickly search buildings and other areas of possible concealment, and save much time. His image, powers of detection and speed of foot are surely enough to justify his use, but in addition to these assets, some police dogs have a desire and ability to follow a track that experience has shown them might lead to a satisfying fight. It's when a police dog has this latter quality that big mistakes are often made in handling.

When such a dog is brought into a situation where a suspect has fled, the handler will often try to start him as he would for a building-search, playing percentages and believing that sheer desire will provide the skill to find and follow the right track. Often, sending a dog in the "general direction" is to direct him without focus to where he will work high-headed on airborne scents, and his natural ability to track is somewhat wasted. Natural ability and drive cannot substitute for the skill acquired through methodical training and practice.

The following anology conveys that truth. Probably every policeman who uses a gun in defense of others or himself has tremendous desire. But without the acquired skill to use his weapon, that desire might be useless.

A police dog handler who has a real need to add tracking to his dog's abilities would do well to follow the method of motivating and training presented in this book. If you already have a dog that is trained to track reliably, you might find that Chapter 6 will help you to get your dog "scouting for tracks."

Officers who are called upon to use a dog in seeking lost persons should find Chapter 6 useful. It offers an example of how to handle a correctly trained tracking dog on a search for a lost person. Many of the same techniques for avoiding the problems in a "stamped out area" and estimating probabilities, will be just as useful in finding and starting the track of a suspect as they are when seeking a lost person. But once the track is found, you can expect some radical differences between the track of a person who is lost and that of the suspect who is trying to avoid capture.

The travel path of a lost and confused person will be

Work and practice in harness will not lessen a dog's ability to work free during those times he is needed for a hot pursuit, when lots of cover and escape routes could give an officer a problem. "Murf", the Bouvier pictured here, is a member of the Montclair, California police department. He is handled by Officer Wes Fowler. In addition to being an effective dog "on the street", "Murf" has been a top dog in Police Dog Trials.

unpredictable as to pattern and direction, but ordinarily he will avoid difficult obstacles and obvious threats such as thorny brush and treacherous footing. The fact that a lost person will follow the easiest and most inviting path can be part of the logic you will use when you scout for a track.

But remember the other factors, such as scent-drift and peculiarities of terrain. Uneven ground and obstacles can divert air currents, and influence a dog to trail airborne scent some distance from the actual track. Rely on your dog in such cases. There are times when a logical mind must defer to a dog's good nose. The more you practice working a variety of environments, the more you will understand the sign you find, and the better you will read your dog's responses.

In following a suspect's sign, you will find that the number of possible routes he might choose to avoid capture is almost infinite. Often a tracking dog can help to sort out the right route. Even in the case where a burglar leaves the rear of a store and crosses a parking lot to a car, it can be useful for an officer to know where the car was probably parked, and thus deduce where it left the lot. If the exit leads to a one-way street, a deduction can be made as to the initial direction of departure. A man and dog team arriving at the exit of a store in response to a night alarm, has a good chance to start and follow a track from that point out onto the lot. At night, when most store burglaries occur, the track the dog finds could well be that of the burglar.

Obviously, the tracking-dog's value is maximized when tracks start in an area removed from cars and streets, and where bushes and other natural cover exists.

Household burglaries are often different than the "grab-and-go" store jobs. Homes are usually not as well cased as stores and the variety of articles, and the places where they are hidden, cause a burglar to spend more time in his search. Houses are seldom checked by police as is the case with stores, and hours sometimes pass before the burglaries are discovered.

In many such cases, with the fewer conflicting tracks and the presence of lawns, a tracking-dog can have significant value, even when there is little chance of tracking the burglar to where he can be apprehended. If the condition of the doors and windows shows that the entrance and exit were made on a particular side of the house, there is a high probability that any recent track from the exit area would be that of the burglar. In such circumstances, though a dog might not be able to track the burglar to where he could be apprehended, anything a dog can do to indicate the way a suspect went after leaving the yard could be important. A policeman who knows the probable path of a suspect can focus his inquiries on those persons who might have seen him walking from the location, or entering a car. To be able to aim a search in the right direction will generally save time and be more productive of facts.

Equal in importance to a dog's good nose is a handler's ability to gather and evaluate facts, such as the paths of any persons who said they had walked from the house to where the suspect would logically have left the yard. This in itself could help to confirm that a track that interested a dog would probably be that of the suspect. Obviously, if your dog tracks away from a yard farther—or in a different direction—than anyone else has traveled, you have confirmed the probability that he's on the track of the suspect. Now watch for footprints and other signs that could give you additional information. Again, the direction of a track and where it ends can have great significance to a sharp policeman.

In such a situation as a house burglary, where yards, parkways and other reasonable tracking terrain surrounds the scene, there could be an advantage in having a dog scout for a track in the way described in Chapter 6 of this book. This is particularly true when there is a limited amount of information as to the time and direction of the burglar's departure, and there are a number of open areas in which he could have traveled.

Most urban areas, with their lack of space, and easy escape routes, have made the use of a tracking-dog more difficult, but there are still situations in which a dog's nose can save time by eliminating possibilities. One of the most common of these is the case where a suspect abandons a car and runs into a park or tries to lose pursuers among landscaped public buildings. In such instances a dog with a good handler can be of tremendous value.

The worth of a capable dog to his department can be greatly enhanced if all of the field personnel would carefully follow two procedures when they see a suspect fleeing from custody:

The first is to accurately relate the position of a tree or another object to the path the fleeing person traveled so that the location of the track can be accurately indicated when a dog is brought to the scene.

Second, until the dog is deployed, try to keep that immediate stretch of ground free from conflicting tracks. Any evidence search should be done after the dog has had his chance. If a dog is started on what is known to be the freshest track in the area, tracks that might cross the one he is following should not confuse him.

"Three feet to the right of that tree," will always mean more than "he went in that direction," especially to a dog handler.

In rural districts where only the general area where a suspect walked is known, and there is small probability of conflicting tracks, use a process of logical elimination, such as presented in Chapter 12 with gathering and using information in order to scout for the track of a lost person. The process of elimination when scouting for the track of the suspect will be the same, although the suspect's evasive actions would result in a track more difficult to follow than the one made by a lost person who wanders around on a path of least resistance.

11

The Bloodhound

A bumbling Bloodhound puppy's inherited propensity to use and believe his nose continues to amaze and amuse those who watch him explore his early environment. But a Bloodhound needs more than a nose he can use and trust to realize his full ability. Various facets of his temperament, such as determination, memory and concentration are important to his work; and it is obvious that rough terrain and other environmental demands make physical qualities of equal importance. Whether a Bloodhound possesses all of these qualities to an equal or greater degree than other breeds used for tracking is much easier argued than proven.

The *Guiness Book of Records* tells of a Doberman Pinscher that followed a track across the African lower veldt for more than 100 miles. This was a continuous track that he followed by scent alone, which is evidence of the dog's ability and physical stamina. There are endless examples of non-Bloodhounds using their powers of scent in the service of man. These facts, and the Bloodhound's rare participation in formal tracking trials, has caused some people to doubt their proficiency. Such doubt is not justified. There is a reason for this lack of interest on the part of Bloodhound enthusiasts. Some of the most field-experienced Bloodhounds with great noses might read a track many feet offwind from where it was laid, or cut loops in a track in a way that would cause a judge to penalize them for such a use of their great ability.

One should not criticize a judge for failure to justify such shortcuts that can result from wind-shifts carrying advanced parts of a track to a good nose. As much as possible the judging of performance must be based on concepts that are not bent according to a judge's experience. Nevertheless, the abilities of some good practical trackers are sometimes regarded as reasons to avoid the strictures of organized trials.

"Is the method this book advocates as well suited to Bloodhounds as it is to other breeds?" is a question sometimes asked. Let's compare it with the way a Bloodhound is often started.

Commonly, the trainers of Bloodhounds and other breeds will encourage a dog to follow a short, easy track for food rewards, then gradually increase the length of the track and the difficulties it poses. The purpose of this pattern is to awaken and develop the dog's natural desire to track. Hopefully, none of these persons believe that, when the dog is brought to the working-level he would track across hot, difficult terrain merely to get a tidbit. They should know he is being fueled by awakened drives.

But they do not know—or do not acknowledge—that the same instincts and desires can be awakened by developing the dog's absolute responsibility to find objects on a track, thus undergirding the dog's instincts and abilities with something stronger than his desire to "do something naturally" when there is nothing else he would sooner do; and insulating him against the distractions that are sure to be on every track. Some of these trainers are not at all concerned with reliability, and are quite content to work in a number of trials before they get a "T." Others "just didn't stop to think."

It's true that the method that makes for the most reliability does require a deep foundation of obedience, and some gullible handlers of Bloodhounds and other breeds believe that obedience training prior to the full development of a dog's natural work drives inhibits his initiative. Review the facts in Chapter 1 of this book. They'll help you debunk the "inhibition" theory.

Yes, the same benefits that this book's methodology brings to other breeds can be brought to the Bloodhound.

12

The Real Thing

IT'S AN EARLY SUMMER AFTERNOON when you get a call from a District Ranger Station, requesting that you bring your tracking-dog to assist in the search for a small boy who strayed from a primitive campsite in a national park. The ranger mentions that a large number of searchers combed the area and found no sign of the boy, and now some feel it would be reasonable to try a dog.

You run a quick check on your light track-pack to be sure you have all essentials. You fill your canteen, and stow it along with the rest of your gear in your car, while your Airedale watches eagerly from the yard gate. On your command, the dog jumps into the car before the gate swings shut behind him.

A half-hour later you stop in a gravel covered parking lot, hemmed by dense forest. A ranger is standing on the edge of the lot, talking with a large group of people. You leave your dog in the car and, with your notebook in hand, join the group to begin one of the most important elements in finding and following the track of a lost person.

The Ranger walks with you down a path that leads to an area where campsites are hardly visible among the trees and tall ferns. He points to where the path turns from sight several hundred feet past the last secluded campsite. "That's where the boy was last seen. His parents didn't know the path ends right after that turn. When he disappeared, they thought he was still on the path and weren't concerned. Later, when his mother walked down to get him, she found the path ended in an area where everything looks alike. There wasn't a trace of him. The parents and others in the camp area scoured around in all directions from the end of the path. They didn't find any sign, and might not have recognized it if they did. They stomped the area out before they called me, so I don't know how I can point you at a starting place."

"There's a way," you tell the Ranger. "First of all, I want to talk to everyone who looked for the boy, particularly his parents."

The two of you return to the parking lot, and at the suggestion of the Ranger, the entire group gathers close together, some sitting on the rail that encloses the area and others leaning against their cars, while the parents give you every significant fact on the lost boy.

You ask for his height so you might verify a track by means of a footprint that a boy his size might make. You ask about all of his general physical abilities, such as endurance in walking so you can estimate how far he would be able to walk since he disappeared. To support any estimates you might make, you inquire as to his temperament. Would he be inclined to bull ahead when he realized he was lost or would he give up and stop and cry. When did he last eat? When you finish your notes on his physical and mental profile, you ask a final question of his parents.

"As actually as you can say, what time did the boy disappear?" *You make the parents understand the importance of knowing the maximum time the boy could have been moving.*

With all the information the parents can supply in your notebook, you turn to the others in the group. You ask them to estimate as accurately as possible how long each of them searched. The general direction they searched is another question, and whether any of them worked in a straight course or meandered from one favorable bit of terrain to another. You explain to them how this information can help you in scouting for a track.

Your final questions are put to the Ranger. Your questions to him are mostly concerned with any features of the area that would be inviting to a frightened, irrational child. In any of the most likely directions of travel what would be the maximum distance a boy could have traveled by this time?

On a leaf of your notebook, the Ranger sketches several landmarks that would be approximately within a radius of three miles from where the boy disappeared.

You carefully add each fact to your notes, knowing that a slight detail can help you start your dog logically and help you to verify a track.

"Are you sure he couldn't have gone farther than three miles from the starting point in the elapsed time" you ask the Ranger.

"Positively. Even if he walked in a straight line, and that would be almost impossible."

"What about the searchers?" you ask him. "Not a one of them said he went out that far."

"They're probably correct," the Ranger answers. "We've found that generally a searcher won't walk as far in a given time as the one he's hunting would. A searcher stops and looks around a lot."

"Good," you tell him. "That means if I start about three miles out from the end of the path, I'll be past the stomped out area, and probably won't have more than a couple of competing tracks to sort out from the boy's track."

You explain to the Ranger the way you will scout for the boy's track, instead of wandering around like a lost soul looking for a dropped object. His face lights up and he nods as you point out the high percentages your approach will provide. He points toward the narrow, brush-flanked service road that starts near the Ranger Station and runs between the forest and some cleared ground to the East.

"I like the way you've got it figured. Load your dog and gear into my Jeep. I'll take you three miles up the road for your start."

Ten minutes later the Ranger stops the Jeep near a huge pine stump. "An East to West line from here would pass a good three miles north of the path where the boy was last seen." He holds out his hand. "The best of luck to you and your dog. A lot depends on the two of you."

A sharp turn takes the Jeep out over the low brush and back onto the road.

You walk a short distance into the timber, and stop to zero your pedometer and arrange your gear. The country before you is covered with big firs and cedars and occasional brush patches. Much of the ground is carpeted with dry conifer needles. It would be easy to walk in any direction. An inexperienced person might believe the uncomplicated terrain would be favorable to tracking, which could be a big mistake. There are no physical barriers or impassable cover to channel a lost person in a limited direction. A person lost in a steep-sided western canyon would have to move either up or down the canyon. Though such an area might be difficult to traverse, the problem of a general direction would be half that posed by a totally accessible area. A person lost in an area bounded by a river or other physical obstacles has fewer options of directions to travel. You know, as you face the open timber, that you are about to search the kind of area where the slightest whim or panic could send a person in any direction, including a circle.

You put the harness on your dog and attach the line, and down him as part of the usual starting-pattern. You give the command, "Find it," and follow the questing dog out into the timber.

As you walk along through the summer's heat, you review the information you have on the problem. There were some positive components. If the boy had veered out onto the service road, he would have stayed on it. If he had turned in the wrong direction, the Ranger would have found him on one of his drives up the road. You are sure that Bobby is somewhere in the forest, and almost certainly within a three-mile radius of the path where he disappeared. How far out from that point and at what angle is the problem you and your dog have to solve. But the known facts and your skills in deduction will reduce the search to a limited and reasonable perimeter. You check your watch, compass and pedometer. All three will be of help as you scout for a track in an arc that keeps at least three miles from the path's end. If you don't cut the boy's track on the first arc, you'll have to make another decision.

Within a quarter of an hour of steady walking, you estimate you have passed a point that would be straight north of the camp area. Now you sight on trees and other markers and check them against your compass heading to help you manage a course that arcs slightly to the left. Your dog is panting but continues to keep a slight tension on the line as you move along, sure that his nose will pick up any track on your course, and hoping it will be that of the boy.

You enter a wide area where the ground is smooth, almost free from cover, and the trees are far apart. Halfway across the open expanse, your dog stops. Then, nose close to the ground, he begins to move slowly at a right angle to the way you were heading. For a few hundred feet, he keeps the line taut and his nose close to what appears to be a sustained ground scent. You check the ground he works for visual verification of a track. Where a streak of fine gravel roughens the surface, you notice a few pebbles have been scuffed from place. You breathe a bit faster as you see your dog is right on a track. Then, in the middle of the strip is something you would rather not see. It's a deep impression of a man's shoe. At least one person other than the boy had walked this far from the path.

You move up to your dog and praise him in a way that tells him he did good, but that track is finished. You put the collar and leash on him to make it clear there'll be a break until you start him scouting again.

You go back to the point where the dog turned right to follow the man's track, and then take a few steps on your former westwardly course, and again equip the dog with harness and longe. You start him scouting again and continue your shallow arc to the southwest for another hour without cutting another track. Then you become aware of a distant murmuring sound that comes over the rustling of the forest and the sound of Ben's panting. It's the sound of a heavy truck, and as you stop and listen you can make out the lighter hum of cars. A look at the sketch the Ranger made is reason to rationalize carefully. It's obvious that the time you've spent walking and the arc you've made has taken you far enough west to hear traffic on the highway that runs west of the camp area.

If, when he left the path, the boy had angled to the west he, too, would have been able to hear the traffic noise and be guided to the highway; and his whereabouts would have been known and reported by now. But if he had walked approximately north he would not have heard the sounds and would still be somewhere between the first arc you had worked and the camp.

Percentages would favor turning south for a short distance and then starting a return arc back toward the service road. If your rationale is right, and the boy has continued to move on a northerly course during the time you have been working, such a return arc should cut his track. But if he stopped from confusion or exhaustion, still another arc might be needed to pick up his track. And even if your plan is sound, there is a factor that could complicate its employment.

The shadows that streak the occasional clearing are getting long. It will soon be dark. A dog's nose does not depend on "seeing," but it's harder for his handler to read him and to verify a track in the dark. The effect of darkness on the boy would be either of two extremes. Terror might cause him to give up and stop moving. Or it might cause him to panic and move about erratically and lay a track full of turns that could slow your dog.

You check your pedometer and compass, and then, with your dog scouting in front of you, go a quarter of a mile straight south. You then make another left turn and start an arc in a shallow northeasterly direction that runs roughly parallel to the course you followed away from the service road. To follow a return course that would take you closer to the campsite might lead into a maze of tracks left by searchers, and there would be no time left to sort them out before dark.

By the time you've worked a half mile on the return course, a cool evening breeze moves against your left side. You estimate you are getting close to a line from the campsite to the point where Ben hit the man track, and wonder if he will hit it again. The coolness seems a signal for increased activity in the forest, and every few hundred feet a rabbit materializes and streaks through the brush. You hear a rattle in a dry windfall and turn to see a doe bound from her cover and angle away from you. You know there must be a fawn under the windfall. Ben freezes momentarily at the doe's appearance, then goes back to work as though the sight reminded him of his responsibility. You are glad your training sacked him off of distractions. In this primitive environment, a handler could become frustrated trying to read a dog that wanted to investigate animal tracks.

You stop to give your dog a short drink, then start him out again. Almost immediately he stops, and, nose to the ground moves off slowly to the left in a pattern that you've read many times. Then you stop him smoothly. On a bare spot that he has worked is a footprint. A big print of a man. It doesn't surprise you that the heel mark is the same as the one you saw on the track to the north.

The fact that you stopped him, or perhaps the memory of being taken off that scent where he had found it farther up the track, causes Ben to show no further interest in it.

Once more you cue your dog and move out. Within the next hundred feet you're moving through a jungle of ferns that brush your shoulders and hide the dog from sight. Suddenly the light tension that keeps the line off the ground slackens, then grows taut.

You stoop below the canopy of fern tops and see your dog checking the ground scent and moving slowly to the north. You have to walk with a stoop to keep him in view, but realize that a small child could easily walk upright beneath the canopy. If the dog has a fresh track, it could be the one you want. Ben's nose leads the way past some small ferns that have been broken. You feel that chill known to a hunter, a prospector and a tracker when their senses tell them they are close to a find.

The fine layer of debris on the ground thins out to reveal bare earth, indistinct in the gloom of the forest. You take your flashlight from the pack and hold the beam at a low angle. A small heel print appears on the ground Ben has worked. Then another print. Ben's actions become more intense. He tracks within a few feet of a huge log, then stops abruptly, nose straight out. A small figure is sitting on the mossy ground, his head leaning back against the log. He is motionless, the expression on his face not visible in the gloom, and his stillness doesn't tell whether he is frightened or asleep.

"Bobby," you say softly, from a distance. "Ben and I are here to take you back to camp. First, I'll give you a drink and a peanut bar. Then we'll go see your Mom and Dad."

As you draw closer you can see the boy grinning. He drinks thirstily and takes the bar with an enthusiastic, "Thank you."

You remove Ben's harness as part of telling him his job is done; but put him on the line and collar to prevent any off-lead celebration in the tracking environment. He'll get his big celebration in another area.

A slow walk of a mile takes you east to the service road, south of where you started scouting. It's dark when you and the boy, who holds firmly to your hand, start down the road. Within minutes you see headlights, and stand waiting while the Ranger turns his Jeep around. He gets out to shake your hand warmly, then lifts Bobby into the Jeep.

Every now and then as you bump along, the Ranger taps out a happy rhythm on the horn.

Back at the campsite, you're glad for the tearful thanks the boy's parents shower on you and your dog. And you're equally grateful your dog had a motivation of responsibility that kept him going with a total disregard for the distractions a tracking dog encounters.

APPENDIX

American Kennel Club Rules and Regulations for Tracking Dog and Tracking Dog Excellent Titles

CHAPTER 7
TRACKING

Section 1. **Tracking Test.** This test shall be for dogs not less than six months of age, and must be judged by two judges. A dog may continue to compete in this test after it has won the title "T. D." or "T. D. X." With each entry form for a licensed or member tracking test for a dog that has not passed an AKC tracking test there must be filed an original written statement, dated within six months of the date the test is to be held, signed by a person who has been approved by The American Kennel Club to judge tracking tests, certifying that the dog is considered by him to be ready for such a test. These original statements cannot be used again and must be submitted to The American Kennel Club with the entry forms. Written permission to waive or modify this requirement may be granted by The American Kennel Club in unusual circumstances. Tracking tests are open to all dogs that are otherwise eligible under these Regulations.

This test cannot be given at a dog show or obedience trial. The duration of this test may be one day or more within a 15 day period after the original date in the event of an unusually large entry or other unforeseen emergency, provided that the change of date is satisfactory to the exhibitors affected.

Section 2. **T.D. Title.** The American Kennel Club will issue a Tracking Dog certificate to a registered dog, and will permit the use of the letters "T.D." after the name of each dog which has been certified by the two judges to have passed a licensed or member tracking test in which at least three dogs actually participated.

The owner of a dog holding both the U.D. and T.D. titles may use the letters "U.D.T." after the name of the dog, signifying "Utility Dog Tracker."

Section 3. **Tracking.** The tracking test must be performed with the dog on leash, the length of the track to be not less than 440 yards nor more than 500 yards, the scent to be not less than one half hour nor more than two hours old and that of a stranger who will leave an inconspicuous glove or wallet, dark in color, at the end of the track where it must be found by the dog and picked up by the dog or handler. The article must be approved in advance by the judges. The tracklayer will follow the track which has been staked out with flags a day or more earlier, collecting all the flags on the way with the exception of one flag at the start of the track and one flag about 30 yards from the start of the track to indicate the direction of the track; then deposit the article at the end of the track and leave the course, proceeding straight ahead at least 50 feet. The tracklayer must wear his own shoes which, if not having leather soles, must have uppers of fabric or leather. The dog shall wear a harness to which is attached a leash between 20 and 40 feet in length. The handler shall follow the dog at a distance of not less than 20 feet, and the dog shall not be guided by the handler. The dog may be restrained by the handler, but any leading or guiding of the dog constitutes grounds for calling the handler off and marking the dog "Failed." A dog may, at the handler's option, be given one, and only one, second chance to take the scent between the two flags, provided it has not passed the second flag.

Section 4. **Tracking Tests.** A person who is qualified to judge Obedience Trials is not necessarily capable of judging a tracking test. Tracking judges must be familiar with the various conditions that may exist when a dog is required to work a scent trail. Scent conditions, weather, lay of the land, ground cover, and wind, must be taken into consideration, and a thorough knowledge of this work is necessary.

One or both of the judges must personally lay out each track, a day or so before the test, so as to be completely familiar with the location of the track, landmarks and ground conditions. At least two of the right angle turns shall be well out in the open where there are no fences or other boundaries to guide the dog. No part of any track shall follow along any fence or boundary within 15 yards of such boundary. The track shall include at least two right angle turns and should include more than two such turns so that the dog may be observed working in different wind directions. Acute angle turns should be avoided whenever possible. No conflicting tracks shall be laid. No track shall cross any body of water. No part of any track shall be laid within 75 yards of any other track. In the case of two tracks going in opposite directions, however, the first flags of these tracks may be as close as 50 yards from each other. The judges shall make sure that the track is no less than 440 yards nor more than 500 yards and that the tracklayer is a stranger to the dog in each case. It is the judges' responsibility to instruct the tracklayer to insure that each track is properly laid and that each tracklayer carries a copy of the chart with him in laying the track. The judges must approve the article to be left at the end of each track, must make sure that it is thoroughly impregnated with the tracklayer's scent, and must see that the tracklayer's shoes meet the requirements of these regulations.

There is no time limit provided the dog is working, but a dog that is off the track and is clearly not working should not be given any minimum time, but should be marked Failed. The handler may not be given any assistance by the judges or anyone else. If a dog is not tracking it shall not be marked Passed even though it may have found the article. In case of unforseen circumstances, the judges may in rare cases, at their own discretion, give a handler and his dog a second chance on a new track. A track for each dog entered shall be plotted on the ground by one or both judges not less than one day before the test, the track being marked by flags which the tracklayer can follow readily on the day of the test. A chart of each track shall be made up in duplicate, showing the approximate length in yards of each leg, and major landmarks and boundaries, if any. Both of these charts shall be marked at the time the dog is tracking, one by each of the judges, so as to show the approximate course followed by the dog. The judges shall sign their charts and show on each whether the dog "Passed" or "Failed," the time the tracklayer started, the time the dog started and finished tracking, a brief description of ground, wind and weather conditions, the wind direction, and a note of any steep hills or valleys.

The Club or Tracking Test Secretary, after a licensed or member tracking test, shall forward the two copies of the judges' marked charts, the entry forms with certifications attached, and a marked and certified copy of the catalog pages or sheets listing the dogs entered in the tracking test, to The American Kennel Club so as to reach its office within seven days after the close of the test.

CHAPTER 7A

Section 1. **Tracking Dog Excellent Test.** This test shall be for dogs that have earned the title T.D., and must be judged by two judges. The maximum number of dogs two judges may be asked to test in one day is five. Dogs that have earned this title T.D.X. may continue to compete. This test cannot be given at a dog show or obedience trial. In the event of an unforeseen emergency, the duration of this test may be more than one day but within a 15 day period after the original date provided that the extension of the test is satisfactory to the exhibitors affected.

Section 2. **T.D.X.** The American Kennel Club will issue a Tracking Dog Excellent certificate to a registered dog, and will permit the use of the letters "T.D.X." after the name of each dog that has been certified by the two judges to have passed a licensed or member club. Tracking Dog Excellent Test in which at least two dogs actually participated.

The owner of the dog holding the "U.D." and "T.D.X." titles may use the letters "U.T.D.X." after the name ofthe dog, signifying "Utility Dog Tracker Excellent."

Section 3. **The T.D.X. Track.** The Tracking Dog Excellent Test must be performed with dog on leash. The length of the track shall not be less than 800 yards nor more than 1000 yards. The scent shall be not less than three hours nor more than four hours old and must be that of a stranger. The actual track, laid earlier, shall be crossed at two widely separated places by more recent tracks.

Four personal dissimilar articles, well impregnated with the tracklayer's scent, will be dropped by the tracklayer at designated points directly on the track. The articles must be approved in advance by the judges.

At a point more than 75 yards from the start of the track the tracklayer will be given a map of the track. He will place one article at the starting flag then follow the track which has been staked out with flags, a day or more earlier. Along the way of the actual track he will collect all but the first flag. He will drop the remaining three articles directly on the track at points designated on the map. The articles shall not be dropped within 30 yards of a turn or cross track. After dropping the last article the tracklayer will proceed straight ahead for at least 30 yards and then leave the field.

One hour to one hour and a half after the actual tracklaying has been completed the judges will instruct two people, strangers to the dog, to start from a given point, walking side by side about four feet apart, and follow each of the two cross tracks which have been staked out with flags a day or more earlier, collecting all of the flags along the way.

While tracking the dog shall wear a harness to which is attached a leash 20 feet to 40 feet in length. To avoid entanglement the leash may be dropped during the tracking but must be retrieved. The dog must be under the handler's control at all times. At the start of the track the dog will be given ample time to take the scent and begin tracking. No guidance of any kind is to be employed by the handler while starting the dog on the track. Since there is no second flag in this test, the handler must wait for the dog to commit itself before he leaves the starting flag. Once the handler has left the starting flag the test has begun and shall not be restarted. The handler may pick up the article at the starting flag and may use it, as well as subsequent articles, to give the scent to the dog while on the track. Where obstacles, barriers or terrain demand, a handler may aid the dog, but any leading or guiding of the dog shall constitute grounds for calling the handler off and marking the dog "Failed."

Should the dog follow one of the cross tracks for distance of more than 50 yards, the dog is to be marked "Failed." The dog must follow the track and either indicate or retrieve the second, third and fourth articles. In order for the dog to be marked "Passed," these articles must be presented to the judge, when the track is completed.

Section 4. **Essentials for a T.D.X. Test,** AKC tracking judges may be approved to judge this test. Such judges must have experience with advanced tracking and be familiar with conditions that present themselves when a dog is reguired to work a scent trail. Scent conditions such as weather, age, terrain, ground cover changes, natural as well as man-made obstacles, cross tracks, streams and roads must be taken into consideration when judging advanced tracking.

Both judges must personally lay out each track a day or so before the test in order to be completely familiar with the location of the track, landmarks and ground conditions. The track shall be not less than 800 yards nor more than 1000 yards and shall contain at least three turns and two widely separated double cross tracks. The cross tracks shall intersect the actual track at right angles. All types of terrain and cover, including gulleys, plowed land, woods and vegetation of any density may be used. Natural obstacles such as streams or man-made obstacles such as hedgerows fences, bridges, or lightly traveled roads may also be used. No portion of any track, including the tracklayer's escape route or the escape route of the cross tracklayers, may be within 75 yards of any other track.

It is the judges' responsibility to instruct the tracklayer and the cross tracklayers so as to insure that each track is properly laid and that they each carry a copy of the chart with them while laying track.

For each dog entered a track shall be plotted on the grounds by both of the judges, not less than one day before the test, the track being marked by flags which the tracklayer can readily follow on the day of the test. A chart of each track shall be made up in duplicate, showing the approximate length in yards of each leg, major landmarks and boundaries, and clearly defined points for dropping the three remaining articles. Both of these charts shall be marked at the time the dog is tracking, one by each of the judges, to show the approximate course followed by the dog. The judges shall sign their charts and show on each whether the dog "Passed" or "Failed." The judges shall also mark the time the tracklayer started, the time the cross tracklayers started, the times the dog started and finished tracking, a brief description of ground, weather conditions and wind direction.

Four personal dissimilar articles shall be dropped on the track. Only the last article may be a glove or wallet. The first article shall be placed at the starting flag and shall be clearly visible to the handler. The 2nd, 3rd, and 4th articles shall be dropped directly on the track at wide intervals and should not be visible to the handler from a distance of 20 feet. The drops shall be clearly marked on the chart and shall not be within 30 yards of a turn or a cross track. Articles must be small enough to be easily carried by the handler while completing the track. The judges must approve the four articles to be used making sure that they have been thoroughly impregnated with the tracklayer's scent. The tracklayer must wear his own shoes which may be of any material. Particular attention should be paid to instructing cross tracklayers and to keeping them away from the start of the actual track.

There is no time limit provided the dog is working. A dog that clearly is not working should not be given any minimum time, but should be marked "Failed." The handler may not be given any assistance by the judges or anyone else. If the dog is not tracking, it shall not be marked "Passed," even though it may find the articles.

In the event of peculiar or unusual circumstances, the judges may, at their own discretion, in rare cases, give a handler and dog a second chance on a new track.

Upon the completion of a licensed or member Tracking Dog Excellent Test, the secretary of the club shall forward to The American Kennel Club, so as to reach the AKC office within seven days after the close of the test, the following:

a. Two copies of the judges' marked charts.

b. Entry forms.

c. Marked and certified copy of the catalog pages or sheets listing dogs entered in this test.

BIBLIOGRAPHY

ALL OWNERS of pure-bred dogs will benefit themselves and their dogs by enriching the knowledge of breeds and of canine care, training, breeding, psychology and other important aspect of dog management. The following list of books covers further reading recommended by judge veterinarians, breeders, trainers and other authorities. Books may be obtained at the finer boo stores and pet shops, or through Howell Book House Inc., publishers, New York.

Breed Books

AFGHAN HOUND, Complete — *Miller & Gilbert*
AIREDALE, New Complete — *Edwards*
AKITA, Complete — *Linderman & Funk*
ALASKAN MALAMUTE, Complete — *Riddle & Seeley*
BASSET HOUND, Complete — *Braun*
BEAGLE, New Complete — *Noted Authorities*
BLOODHOUND, Complete — *Brey & Reed*
BOXER, Complete — *Denlinger*
BRITTANY SPANIEL, Complete — *Riddle*
BULLDOG, New Complete — *Hanes*
BULL TERRIER, New Complete — *Eberhard*
CAIRN TERRIER, Complete — *Marvin*
CHESAPEAKE BAY RETRIEVER, Complete — *Cherry*
CHIHUAHUA, Complete — *Noted Authorities*
COCKER SPANIEL, New — *Kraeuchi*
COLLIE, New — *Official Publication of the Collie Club of America*
DACHSHUND, The New — *Meistrell*
DALMATIAN, The — *Treen*
DOBERMAN PINSCHER, New — *Walker*
ENGLISH SETTER, New Complete — *Tuck, Howell & Graef*
ENGLISH SPRINGER SPANIEL, New — *Goodall & Gasow*
FOX TERRIER, New Complete — *Silvernail*
GERMAN SHEPHERD DOG, New Complete — *Bennett*
GERMAN SHORTHAIRED POINTER, New — *Maxwell*
GOLDEN RETRIEVER, New Complete — *Fischer*
GORDON SETTER, Complete — *Look*
GREAT DANE, New Complete — *Noted Authorities*
GREAT DANE, The—Dogdom's Apollo — *Draper*
GREAT PYRENEES, Complete — *Strang & Giffin*
IRISH SETTER, New Complete — *Eldredge & Vanacore*
IRISH WOLFHOUND, Complete — *Starbuck*
JACK RUSSEL TERRIER, Complete — *Plummer*
KEESHOND, Complete — *Peterson*
LABRADOR RETRIEVER, Complete — *Warwick*
LHASA APSO, Complete — *Herbel*
MINIATURE SCHNAUZER, Complete — *Eskrigge*
NEWFOUNDLAND, New Complete — *Chern*
NORWEGIAN ELKHOUND, New Complete — *Wallo*
OLD ENGLISH SHEEPDOG, Complete — *Mandeville*
PEKINGESE, Quigley Book of — *Quigley*
PEMBROKE WELSH CORGI, Complete — *Sargent & Harper*
POODLE, New Complete — *Hopkins & Irick*
POODLE CLIPPING AND GROOMING BOOK, Complete — *Kalstone*
ROTTWEILER, Complete — *Freeman*
SAMOYED, Complete — *Ward*
SCHIPPERKE, Official Book of — *Root, Martin, Kent*
SCOTTISH TERRIER, New Complete — *Marvin*
SHETLAND SHEEPDOG, The New — *Riddle*
SHIH TZU, Joy of Owning — *Seranne*
SHIH TZU, The (English) — *Dadds*
SIBERIAN HUSKY, Complete — *Demidoff*
TERRIERS, The Book of All — *Marvin*
WEST HIGHLAND WHITE TERRIER, Complete — *Marvin*
WHIPPET, Complete — *Pegram*
YORKSHIRE TERRIER, Complete — *Gordon & Bennett*

Breeding

ART OF BREEDING BETTER DOGS, New — *Onstott*
BREEDING YOUR OWN SHOW DOG — *Seranne*
HOW TO BREED DOGS — *Whitney*
HOW PUPPIES ARE BORN — *Prine*
INHERITANCE OF COAT COLOR IN DOGS — *Little*

Care and Training

COUNSELING DOG OWNERS, Evans Guide for — *Evan*
DOG OBEDIENCE, Complete Book of — *Saunder*
NOVICE, OPEN AND UTILITY COURSES — *Saunder*
DOG CARE AND TRAINING FOR BOYS AND GIRLS — *Saunder*
DOG NUTRITION, Collins Guide to — *Collin*
DOG TRAINING FOR KIDS — *Benjam*
DOG TRAINING, Koehler Method of — *Koehle*
DOG TRAINING Made Easy — *Tucke*
GO FIND! Training Your Dog to Track — *Dav*
GUARD DOG TRAINING, Koehler Method of — *Koehle*
MOTHER KNOWS BEST—The Natural Way to Train Your Dog — *Benjami*
OPEN OBEDIENCE FOR RING, HOME AND FIELD, Koehler Method of — *Koehl*
STONE GUIDE TO DOG GROOMING FOR ALL BREEDS — *Stor*
SUCCESSFUL DOG TRAINING, The Pearsall Guide to — *Pears*
TOY DOGS, Kalstone Guide to Grooming All — *Kalstor*
TRAINING THE RETRIEVER — *Kersl*
TRAINING TRACKING DOGS, Koehler Method of — *Koehle*
TRAINING YOUR DOG—Step by Step Manual — *Volhard & Fish*
TRAINING YOUR DOG TO WIN OBEDIENCE TITLES — *Mors*
TRAIN YOUR OWN GUN DOG, How to — *Good*
UTILITY DOG TRAINING, Koehler Method of — *Koehl*
VETERINARY HANDBOOK, Dog Owner's Home — *Carlson & Gif*

General

AKC'S WORLD OF THE PURE-BRED DOG — *American Kennel Cl*
CANINE TERMINOLOGY — *Spi*
COMPLETE DOG BOOK, The — *Official Publication American Kennel Cl*
DOG IN ACTION, The — *Ly*
DOG BEHAVIOR, New Knowledge of — *Pfaffenberg*
DOG JUDGE'S HANDBOOK — *Tietj*
DOG JUDGING, Nicholas Guide to — *Nichol*
DOG PEOPLE ARE CRAZY — *Ridc*
DOG PSYCHOLOGY — *Whitn*
DOGSTEPS, Illustrated Gait at a Glance — *Elli*
DOG TRICKS — *Haggerty & Benjam*
ENCYCLOPEDIA OF DOGS, International — *Dangerfield, Howell & Ridc*
EYES THAT LEAD—Story of Guide Dogs for the Blind — *Tuck*
FRIEND TO FRIEND—Dogs That Help Mankind — *Schwa*
FROM RICHES TO BITCHES — *Shattu*
HAPPY DOG/HAPPY OWNER — *Sieg*
IN STITCHES OVER BITCHES — *Shattu*
JUNIOR SHOWMANSHIP HANDBOOK — *Brown & Mas*
MY TIMES WITH DOGS — *Fletch*
OUR PUPPY'S BABY BOOK (blue or pink)
SUCCESSFUL DOG SHOWING, Forsyth Guide to — *Fors*
TRIM, GROOM & SHOW YOUR DOG, How to — *Saund*
WHY DOES YOUR DOG DO THAT? — *Bergm*
WILD DOGS in Life and Legend — *Rid*
WORLD OF SLED DOGS, From Siberia to Sport Racin — *Coppin*